SOCIETY WOMEN OF SHAKESPEARE'S TIME

ELIZABETH LADY RUSSELL
From a portrait at Bisham Abbey
Reproduced by the kind permission of Lady Vansittart-Neale

SOCIETY WOMEN
OF SHAKESPEARE'S TIME
BY VIOLET A. WILSON
WITH TWELVE ILLUSTRATIONS

KENNIKAT PRESS
Port Washington, N. Y./London

SOCIETY WOMEN OF SHAKESPEARE'S TIME

First published in 1924
Reissued in 1970 by Kennikat Press
Library of Congress Catalog Card No: 73-113370
ISBN 0-8046-1040-1

Manufactured by Taylor Publishing Company   Dallas, Texas

PREFACE

SHAKESPEARE'S heroines undoubtedly had their origin in the society women of the time. The dramatist may not have come into close social contaćt with the great Elizabethan ladies, but he had ample opportunity of knowing them well, both by sight and reputation. Daily he would pass them in the London streets, driving in their resplendent coaches, or walking afoot attended by pages and ushers. At Court performances they formed an appreciative audience of the author's plays, and frequently sent for the Globe players to give performances at their private houses.

Shakespeare had no lack of interesting women to study for his portrait gallery; learned women like Lady Russell; clever stateswomen as Lady Raleigh and Lady Warwick; vengeful women like Lady Shrewsbury and Lady Somerset; a devout one in Lady Hoby, and a devoted mother in her sister-in-law, Lady Sidney. Beautiful, vivacious Lady Rich, impetuous Lady Northumberland; humble wives, defiant wives, gentle docile wives like Lady Southampton and Lady Essex.

Not only did Shakespeare know the great ladies well by sight, but their charaćters and concerns were common property in a gossip-loving age, when news-papers were unknown, and news circulated by word of mouth. "How do you? What's the news?" was the accustomed salutation of man to man.

Aubrey says that Shakespeare and Ben Jonson "did gather humours of men dayly whenever they came," frequenting the fashionable throng, walking up and down the middle aisle of St. Paul's Cathedral, "the mint of all famous lies." There rumour circulated freely; true news, false news, good news, bad news, news from the Court, news from abroad, news from the law courts, grave news, scandalous news. A great man's friend, a favourite's minion, a lawyer's clerk, a statesman's secretary, a returned seaman, and a discharged soldier, all brought grist to the mill. For purveyors of domestic chitchat servants from the great houses held pride of place. My lord's gentleman and my lady's page were valued imparters of secret matters. Servants who waited at table had great opportunities like those in *Coriolanus*, who were so quickly surrounded by an ear-tingling crowd:

> *3rd Serv.* . . . I can tell you news; news, you rascals.
> *1st and 2nd Serv.* What, what, what? Let's partake.
> *1st Serv.* But more of thy news.
>
> *Coriolanus*, IV, 5.

Playwrights of the day had no scruple about making use of the news they collected, and by 1601 the topical and personal allusions in their plays had gone to such lengths that the Lords of the Privy Council ordered the Middlesex magistrates to make careful scrutiny of all plays, and censor offensive personalities. Playwrights whose audiences delighted in topical reference, contrived to satisfy the demand by sufficiently obvious allusions, which, though avoiding the law of libel, were perfectly intelligible to the patrons of the Globe Theatre; whilst the actors could no doubt be depended on to mimic the gestures and appearance of intended victims.

In this connection I came across the accounts of two contemporary quarrels which were tried in London and set the whole town talking. Shakespeare undoubtedly knew the parties, and there is so great similarity between the disputes and certain passages in *The Merry Wives of Windsor*, and *Twelfth Night* that I have printed the documents in the Appendix of this book, under the headings of "Shakespeare and a Windsor Quarrel," and "Shakespeare and a Yorkshire Quarrel" (the latter appeared in *The North American Review* for May 1924).

For the illustrations in this volume, I am indebted to the kindness of the Archbishop of Canterbury, the Duke of Bedford, the Duke of Portland, Lord de L'Isle and Dudley, Lady Vansittart Neale; the Bodleian Library, Oxford; the Oxford University Press; St. John's College, Cambridge; Society of Antiquaries of London; the Walpole Society; and to the Marquess of Salisbury for permission to inspect the Hatfield MSS.

BOAR'S HILL HOTEL,   V. A .W.
  BOAR'S HILL,
    OXFORD, *October* 1924.

LIST OF ILLUSTRATIONS

SOCIETY WOMEN OF SHAKESPEARE'S TIME

SOCIETY WOMEN
OF SHAKESPEARE'S TIME

CHAPTER I

"ENGLAND is a paradise for women," so ran
a popular sixteenth-century saying, arising
from the freedom enjoyed by English women
as compared to the position occupied by their
sisters on the Continent. Foreigners, surprised, and
not a little scandalized to find themselves in a country
where "the females have great liberty and are almost
like masters,"[1] whipped out their notebooks to record
the customs of a strange people as exemplified in the
treatment of its wives and daughters.

An impressionable Italian Captain said "their women
are charming, and by nature so mighty pretty as I have
scarcely ever beheld." His opinion was cordially en-
dorsed by another countryman, as "their women are
of marvellous beauty, and wonderfully clever." A susceptible French student even went so far as to say they

[1] Frederick, Duke of Wirtemberg, 1592.

I

were "the greatest beauties in the world, and as fair as alabaster."

Holding the English ladies in such high esteem, visitors were delighted to find that they need not stop at merely beholding. Enraptured foreigners found that, after being introduced to these divinities, they had "even a right to take them by the arm and to kiss them, which is the custom of the country, and if any one does not do so it is regarded and imputed as ignorance."[1] At a dance in this enchanting land the gentleman might say :

> ". . . sweetheart
> I were unmannerly to take you out,
> And not to kiss you."[2]

This privilege, so enthusiastically appreciated by masculine strangers, was suggested by Erasmus as a cure for gout; he urged a friend to think no more of its twinges, but hasten over to England. There he would find "girls with Angels' faces, and so kind and obliging, that you would prefer them to all your Muses. Besides, there is a custom here never to be sufficiently commended. Whenever you come, you are received with a kiss by all; when you take your leave, you are dismissed with kisses; when you return, kisses are repeated. They come to visit you, kisses again; they leave you, you kiss them all round. Should they meet you any-

1 *England as seen by Foreigners*, W. B. Rye.
2 *King Henry VIII*, I, 4.

where, kisses in abundance: in fine, wherever you move, there is nothing but kisses."

Emanuel Van Meteren, a Dutchman, wrote of the English ladies in a more sober strain, for, though admitting they were "beautiful, fair, well-dressed and modest," he was somewhat shocked at their frivolity and lack of domestic qualities:

"They are well-dressed, fond of taking it easy, and commonly leave the care of household matters and drudgery to their servants. . . . In all banquets and feasts they are shown the greatest honour; they are placed at the upper end of the table, where they are the first served; at the lower end they help the men. All the rest of their time they employ in walking and riding, in playing at cards or otherwise, in visiting their friends and keeping company, conversing with their equals (whom they term *gossips*) and their neighbours, and making merry with them at child-births, christenings, churchings and funerals; and all this with the permission and knowledge of their husbands, as such is the custom. Although the husbands often recommend to them the pains, industry, and care of the German or Dutch women, who do what the men ought to do both in the house and in the shops, for which services in England men are employed, nevertheless the women usually persist in retaining their customs "[1]

Not only did the Elizabethan ladies insist on having

[1] *England as seen by Foreigners.*

their own way, but they were already laying claim to equality with men and to ask pertinently, "Why should their liberty than ours be more?" When told a husband should be the bridle of his wife's will, they retorted:

"There's none but asses will be bridled so."[1]

An inexperienced bridegroom might say boastfully:

"I will be master of what is mine own:
She is my goods, my chattels."[2]

A dozen married men would tell him he did not know what he was talking about.

Philip Stubbes, a Puritan pamphleteer who took the female sex severely to task in *The Anatomie of Abuses*, published in 1583, charged them with trying to ape men's fashions. They wore "dublets and jerkins, as men have heer, buttoned up the brest and made with wings, wells and pinioned on the shoulder points, as men's apparel is for all the world; and though this be a kind of attire appropriate only to man, yet they blush not to wear it, and if they could as wel chaunge their sex, and put on the kind of man, as they can weare apparel assigned onely to man, I think they would as verely become men instead, as now they degenerate from godly, sober women in wearing this wanton kind of attire proper onely to man."

Even though the ladies copied men in certain respects they had plenty of purely feminine failings, none of

[1] *The Comedy of Errors*, I, 2.
[2] *The Taming of the Shrew*, III, 2.

4

which escaped the vigilant eye of Master Philip Stubbes. For one thing he was more than doubtful of their complexions; show him a girl whose lovely skin made her look a "queen of curds and cream," and he would not exclaim "most radiant, exquisite, and unmatchable beauty,"[1] as any properly constituted young man would have done. The nearest approach to a compliment such feminine beauty could win from him would be a captious, "excellently done, if God did it all"; and suspicious he would remain even though the lady assured him, "'Tis in grain, sir; 'twill endure wind and weather."[2]

Philip Stubbes knew far more about the secrets of a fashionable lady's toilet than was good for any man. Indignantly he accused them of painting their faces, "whereby they think their beauty is greatly decored." Why they should think so passed his comprehension, and he asked to be enlightened. "Thinkest thou that thou canst make thy self fairer than God, who made all?" Reluctantly Master Stubbes came to the profane conclusion that they really did think so; "else they would never go about to colour their faces with such sibbersawces." But why did they want "to chaunge their naturall face for a painted face, which thou hast made thyself? If thou beest faire, why paintest thou thyself? If thou beest faire, why paintest thou thyself to seeme fairer? and if thou be not faire, why doost thou hypocrittically desire to seeme faire?" It was a question many men asked, but the women scorned to answer.

[1] *Twelfth Night*, I, 5.   [2] *Ibid.*

Then their hair ! in direct defiance of the scriptures which declared authoritatively, "Thou canst not make one hair of black," fashionable ladies daily demonstrated that they could make theirs golden or red if they wished. Further, they were "not simply contented with their own haire, but buy other hayre, dying it what colour they list themselves."

Playwrights knew that dodge as well as Puritans:

> "Look on beauty
> And you shall see 'tis purchas'd by the weight:
> Which therein works a miracle in nature,
> Making them lightest that wear most of it:
> So are those crisped snaky golden locks
> Which make such wanton gambols with the wind,
> Upon supposed fairness, often known
> To be the dowry of a second head,
> The skull that bred them in the sepulchre."[1]

On the top of their very suspicious hair married ladies wore hats "some of this fashion, some of that, and some of this colour, some of that, according to the variable fantasies of their serpentine minds." Other abominations were starched ruffs like cart wheels, and ear-rings.

In the end, after all the trouble the ladies had taken to make themselves attractive, did Philip Stubbes contribute due mead of admiration? He did nothing of the sort; instead, he chid them for "their coynesse in gestures, their minsednes in words and speaches, their

[1] *The Merchant of Venice*, III, 2. Shakespeare lodged for a time with a "tiremaker" in Silver Street, so he knew the secrets of the trade.

gingerlynes in tripping on toes like young goats, their demure nicitie."

Even grandmothers could not be depended upon to set a decorous example. Thomas Nash, another writer, with his own horrified eyes had seen "aged mothers" with "their cheeks sugar-candied and cherry blusht so sweetly," and wearing "nosegayes of yeolow haire on their furious foreheads."[1] After that, the worst could with confidence be predicted for granddaughters.

Puritans might bid these unregenerate women remember, that "women of Africa wear skins; Braslian women go naked"; whilst German women, "nothing like other nations delighting in new fangles," were subject unto their husbands and did all the housework. The Elizabethan ladies laughed at Philip Stubbes and his *Anatomie of Abuses*, but showed no signs of reformation; housework they would not do, and the primitive fashions of the garden of Eve were quite out of date. "The fashion is the fashion,"[2] they said firmly, and ordered the very latest style of gown. Husbands on seeing it, and being expected to escort their ladies out in it, might exclaim in dismay:

"O mercy, God! what masquing stuff is here?
What's this? a sleeve? 'tis like a demi-cannon:
What! up and down, carv'd like an apple-tart?
Here's snip and nip and cut and slish and slash,
Like to a censer in a barber's shop.
Why, what, i' devil's name, tailor, call'st thou this?"[3]

---

[1] *Pierce Penilesse.*
[2] *Much Ado About Nothing*, III, 3.
[3] *The Taming of the Shrew*, IV, 3.

7

To which the tailor in defence would reply that he was bid make it, "according to the fashion of the time," being upheld by his customer, who vowed:

"I never saw a better-fashioned gown,
More quaint, more pleasing, nor more commendable."[1]

Despite their apparent frivolity, Tudor ladies by no means subscribed to Luther's opinion, who when asked, "What becomes women ill?" replied, "There is no gown nor garments that becomes a woman wors than when she will bee wise." The society women of the time were very wise "to saie how many gentlewomen and ladies there are, that besides sound knowledge of the Greeke and Latin toongs are thereto no lesse skilfull in the Spanish, Italian, and French, or in some one of them, it resteth not in me," wrote Harrison in his *Description of England*.

The ladies took their high standard of culture from the Queen, who was said to read more Greek in a day than many dignitaries of the Church read Latin in a week. Lord Burghley himself bore witness to his mistress's statecraft, declaring, "No one of her councillors could tell her what she knew not; and when her Council had said all they could, she could find out a wise counsel beyond theirs, and that there never was anie great consultation about her country at which she was not present to her great profitte and prayse."

Lord Burghley was in a position to speak authoritatively, for he had married as his second wife one of

---

[1] *The Taming of the Shrew*, IV, 3.

the brilliantly clever daughters of Sir Anthony Cooke, famous Greek scholar and tutor to King Edward VI. It was his maxim "that sexes as well as souls are equal in capacity," and he taught his daughters at night what he had taught the prince by day. "His first care," says Lloyd, "was to embrue their infancy with a knowing, serious, and sober religion, which went with them to their graves, and his next to inure their youth to obedience and modesty." Yet whilst teaching his daughters to regard all study as a recreation, he insisted on their devoting part of each day to such housewifery pursuits as needlework, cookery, and the still-room.

Sir Anthony used to say "there were three things before whom he could do no wrong—his prince, his conscience, and his children." His dearest hope being, "that his daughters might have for their husbands complete and perfect men, and that their husbands might be happy in complete women."

In this desire the father was gratified, for despite their celebrated erudition, and a rumour that their tongues were as sharp as their wits, the girls married well. Mildred, justly famed for her Greek translation, became the second wife of Queen Elizabeth's great Minister, Lord Burghley. She proved of valuable assistance to her husband in his political work, and at her death in 1589 he was inconsolable. Anne married another notable man, Sir Nicholas Bacon, the Lord Keeper, and both she and her elder sister were mothers of remarkably clever sons—Sir Robert Cecil and Sir Francis Bacon.

9

Lady Bacon undertook to translate Bishop Jewel's *Apology for the Church of England*, so that it might be accessible to the general public. Archbishop Parker was so delighted with her work that he sent it to be printed, saying he had "thereby done for the best, and in this point used a reasonable policy, that is, to prevent such excuses as her modesty would make in stay of publishing it."

Although she did not make such brilliant marriages as her two sisters, Elizabeth Cooke took a more active part in the contemporary life than did either of them. She outlived two husbands: Sir Thomas Hoby, English Ambassador to France, and John Lord Russell, who died in the lifetime of his father, Francis, second Earl of Bedford, to the grievous distress of his wife, whose highest earthly ambition was to become a Countess. She delighted in ordering pompous funerals, and buried both husbands with due magnificence, afterwards erecting handsome monuments adorned with Greek and Latin verses of her own composing, to their honour at Bisham and Westminster Abbey.

Throughout her widowhood, Lady Russell kept up her classical studies, and translated a Latin book called *A Way of Reconciliation of a Good and Learned Man*. She did not at first intend her work for publication, "but my selfe onely to have some certaintie to leane unto, in a matter so full of controversie, and to yield a reason of my opinion. But since by my lending the copie of mine own hand to a friend, I am bereft thereof by some; And fearing lest after my death it should be

The Lady Hobbei.

ELIZABETH COOKE

From an engraving after Holbein at Bistram Abbey, reproduced by kind permission of Lady Vansittart Neale

printed according to the humors of others, and wrong done to its dead, who in life approved my translation with his own allowance. Therefore dreading, I say, wrong to him above any other I have by anticipation prevented the worst."

Besides writing books, Lady Russell had them presented to her, and Thomas Lodge, who called his patroness the "English Sapho," dedicated his *Margarite of America*, written especially "for ladies delight and ladies honour," to "The noble, learned, and vertuous ladie, the Ladie Russell," wishing her "affluence on earth and felicitie in heaven."

Lodge stated that Lady Russell's "charetie, learning, nobilitie, and vertues" were so famous that they would endure for ever. Therefore, "on the wings of your sacred name," he hoped his book would achieve popularity in the present and immortality for the future.

CHAPTER II

QUEEN ELIZABETH held Lady Russell's ability in high estimation, and writing a letter of condolence to her after the death of Sir Thomas Hoby, when Ambassador to France, she added: "We cannot but let you know, that we hear out of France such singular good reports of your duty well accomplished towards your husband, both living and dead, with other your sober, wise, and discreet behaviour in that Court and Country, that we think it a part of great contentment to us and commendation of our country, that such a gentlewoman hath given so manifest a testimony of virtue in such hard times of adversity. And therefore, though we thought very well of you before, yet shall we hereafter make a more assured account of your virtues and gifts."[1]

Elizabeth did not fulfil this promise till Lady Russell's second widowhood, but then she made amends by appointing her Custodian of Donnington Castle, on the outskirts of Windsor Forest. There was some heart-burning over the matter on the score "that a woman cannot have this Office of the Custody of a castle because it appertains to the war, and is to be executed

[1] *Memoirs of the House of Russell*, J. Wiffen.

by men only."[1] Two such determined women as Queen Elizabeth and Lady Russell were not likely to listen to any arguments based on the inferiority of sex, and the newly appointed custodian held on to her office with a tenacity, not lessened by the complication that whilst she had "the office granted to her of the custody of the castle with all the profits," the right of actual residence in the castle was claimed by the Lord Admiral.[2]

The matter was disputed with much warmth, and no signs of weakening on either side, for years. It involved two lawsuits, and ranged the countryside into opposite camps. When Lady Russell and her partisans met any of the Lord Admiral's adherents, there was certain to be trouble, if not actual bloodshed. In 1594 matters came to a crisis, for the indignant Lady Russell, who had by no means played a pacific part, threatened to make a Star Chamber matter of it, and appealed to the Privy Council through the medium of her nephew, Sir Robert Cecil.

Dowager Lady Elizabeth Russell to the Council[3]

"She has been offered great indignity by Mr. Lovelace, Lieutenant of the Forest and Castle of Windsor

[1] English Law Reports, Sir G. Croke.

[2] Charles Howard, 2nd Baron Effingham, Earl Nottingham, 1596. Commanded Fleet against the Armada, Constable of the Honour and Castle of Windsor, and Keeper of Windsor Forest.

[3] Hatfield MSS. Hist. MS. Com. xiii. Shakespeare refers to this affray in the opening scene of *The Merry Wives of Windsor*. See Appendix, p. 223.

13

under the Lord Admiral. She came early this October to a certain copyhold, to view where certain trees had been cut down by Laurence Manfield and Lovelace's man, and when she came to the house she called for the key, and was answered that Lovelace had it. She commanded the door to be broken open, and found two of Lovelace's men within to keep possession against her, whom she brought home to her house and set them by the heels in her porter's lodge: saying she would teach them to come within her liberties and keep possession against her: Lovelace knowing that no Sheriff has authority to enter or execute any process but by her bailiff, by force of her charter. If she had offered him wrong the law was open to him. Thereupon about two o'clock Lovelace came with 16 halberts and long staves within the gates of her house, which is her castle, broke open the door and locks of the lodge and took out his men. She prays the Council to call Lovelace before them, that he may be committed to prison and fined: to the example of any other who offer the like to any noble woman in her own house, contrary to law and privilege of her liberties held by charter."

Before presenting this document to the Privy Council Sir Robert Cecil consulted Sir Edward Coke, the Attorney-General, as to the justice of his aunt's cause. On October 16th, 1594, the famous lawyer replied:

"I have considered of the state of the cause between my lady Russell and Mr. Lovelace, and of the proceedings on either part, and I take it the Star Chamber is no fit court for my lady to complain in; for, as your honour knoweth, that high court without respect striketh on both sides, and in this case, the causes be so intermixed as on the one day they cannot punish Lovelace, but on the other they must sentence against my lady. For, albeit an honourable lady being so abused as she was could hardly (all circumstances considered) brook such indignities, yet her stocking and imprisonment of his men is not justifiable in law, and seeing there is so great inequality of persons, I would not have them suffer equal punishment. But, if it would please you and other of the honorable lords of her Highness's Council to call Lovelace before you and let him understand the quality of his offence and, if he do not to my lady Russell's satisfaction submit himself, that then it would please you to bind him over till the matter might be more deeply examined, in my opinion it were the best and safest course for my lady."[1]

Lady Russell attributed most of her crosses in life to the fact that her second husband's untimely death had deprived her of the title and privileges of a countess. Indeed she felt it so strongly, that she frequently hinted that she would not be averse to entering the married state a third time, the one essential qualification for the bridegroom being that he should bear a title; it would not even matter if he lacked "four of his five wits";

[1] Hatfield MSS. Hist. MSS. Com. x.

Lady Russell never doubted that she had intelligence enough for both.

The recipient of these confidences was her ladyship's nephew, Sir Robert Cecil, Secretary of State, who as Lord Burghley's infirmities increased was gradually taking over the reins of authority. No one had a higher sense of Sir Robert's importance than his aunt, who, since she could not lay claim to special consideration on the score of being a Countess, did think she had a right to preferential treatment as Mr. Secretary Cecil's aunt.

Lady Russell's letters with two seals over green silk were a constant and often disquieting feature of the young statesman's post-bag. Glancing at the super-scription he could glean some idea of Lady Russell's frame of mind when writing: "Your desolate wronged Aunt." "Your loving Aunt, poor but proud." "Your Aunt that ever deserved the best." "Your honest, plain-dealing Aunt."

The requests, if flattering to Sir Robert's sense of importance, were often embarrassing : Ascanius, a book-seller who lived near Lady Russell in the Black Friars, wanted to be a printer, but the Lord Mayor and his brethren ignored his petition, and Lady Russell desired Cecil to "write to the Mayor to show that it is Her Majesty's pleasure that they should admit him." On another occasion he was to send for a " puisne judge of the Common Pleas, and sharply to take him up," because he had given adverse judgment against Lady Russell, and "my being your Aunt, my place had deserved more regard of justice." Then there was a neighbour who wanted to be a Knight; a dean who had been made a bishop, and wanted to remain a dean. Also Lady Russell had pet candidates for vacant posts, and would request her nephew to "yield your best favour to a godly, honest, and honourable nobleman, the Earl of Kent, to be in the Earl of Huntingdon's place." The Earl was noble; he had no wife; Lady Russell appended a cautionary hint, "I would not have it known to proceed from me, because he is a widower and I a widow."

On another occasion Cecil was requested to rattle up an attorney for upholding the cause of a draper named May, who had dealt "unhonestly, despitefully, and unlawfully " with Mr. Secretary's aunt for a debt of £16. Lady Russell indignantly denied that she owed him anything. She had not dealt at his shop for twelve years past; moreover, she did not run up bills, but always paid ready money. In course of time and argument the sum whittled down to £4, but still Lady Russell refused to pay; "wherein my honour is so touched as if I thought it were offered me because I am a widow, were it to shun inconvenience with a greater mischief purchased to myself do newer cumber like *intestinum vulnus abitum in visceribus meis,* I tell you, Sir—but not the Council table—as lately as I have been at death's door, I would rather marry someone that lacketh one of his five senses rather than carry so great an indignity presumed by so base a fellow for want of a husband honourable. Thus, nephew, may you see, how weak

17

soever my body is made by sickness, my mind is the same it was. . . .

Your desolate Aunt,
E. Russell,
Dowager."

May, the draper, died during the dispute, but his widow, on the advice of her solicitor, continued the suit. Lady Russell wanted the blood of that solicitor, for whatsoever her religion she did most earnestly desire to see her enemies suitably chastened. Sir Robert Cecil, having the privilege of being her ladyship's nephew, was the fittest person to obtain it, and she wrote to tell him her mind: "I am content to refer the matter to yourself, only so that my honour may be repaired with punishment of that base fellow that as a solicitor followeth the cause in the widow's name, and durst presume, contrary to law hitherto in such unordinary manner for my calling, to sue a noble woman to an exigent for denying to pay £4 of a sum that in my soul was but a false pack made between them since her husband's death."

Cecil duly "rattled up the attorney," who afterwards repaired to Lady Russell's house at the Blackfriars, where he endured a very bad half-hour. Her ladyship gave him a severe talking to, being especially insistent to know if his presumption was furthered by her not being a countess. This he stoutly denied, saying he would have done the same "to a widow of any Earl." Somewhat mollified by this admission, Lady Russell eventually compounded the debt.

If Lady Russell was apt in asking favours, she was also ready to confer them on her three nephews, Robert Cecil, and Anthony and Francis Bacon, always providing they were properly appreciative of her kindness, the said nephews being not a little afraid of their aunt's sharp tongue, her anxiety concerning their religious opinions, and her accurate knowledge of their peccadilloes. When Lady Russell got wind of a quarrel between Sir Robert Cecil and Sir William Knollys, Comptroller of the Royal Household, she at once wrote to offer herself as mediator, provided Cecil complied with certain conditions.

"I hear words passed between you and Mr. Comptroller and between the other two Earls. If you will have me come to Court to do you any good offices, who have had ever a natural instinct to be honest and natural in time of trial, howsoever it hath been deserved, let me know your mind, and then, so you procure her Majesty to command my Lord Chamberlain that I may have a convenient lodging within the house, I will come when you desire. Otherwise, upon the least wet of my feet or legs by long clothes or cold, my pate is so subject to rheum that my hearing will be so bad as that I am fit for no company or other place than my own cell.

Your Aunt that ever deserved the best,

E. R.

Dowager."

Cecil himself got into trouble with his aunt when it came to her ears that he was trying to entice away one of her menservants. With considerable asperity did she write unto her presumptuous nephew:

"I have a footman who this morning I hear has been enticed from my service by some secretary of yours and promised £7 by year and 4 suits of apparel. I have great need of a footman, or else being so poor a widow as not able to keep house in the Country as heretofore, I would not have been so great charge with him as I have already bestowed on him, having not been with me scarce a quarter of a year, to the value of above £7 in respect of my 'journeyment' into Wales. And because I hear your footman was here with him this morning, saying that if I would prefer him to you that may command so many will show yourself so religious to a poor lady as to remember who said, 'Thou shalt not covet thy neighbour's house nor his wife nor his servant nor his maids nor anything that is your neighbour's.' "

When not too occupied with mundane affairs, Lady Russell gave anxious thought to posterity. She did not anticipate that either she or hers would be forgotten with the passing of time; still it was well to make quite sure. She had erected handsome monuments to her husbands, and set forth their virtues in various tongues: could she trust her family to do as much for her, and to see no ceremony was omitted at her funeral? Seriously she doubted it. Then there was the question of rank: would she be buried merely as a baroness, she who had so nearly been Countess of Bedford? To endure the humiliation in life was hard enough, surely at death she might at least be a viscountess; she sat down and wrote to Sir William Dethick, Garter King of Arms, on the subject:

"Good Mr. Garter, I pray you, as your leisure doth best serve you, set down advisedly and exactly, in every particular itself, the number of mourners due to my calling, being a Viscountess of birth, with their charge of blacks, and the number of waiting-women for myself, and the women mourners, which with the chief mourner, and her that shall bear the trayne, will be in number ten, beside waiting-women, pages, and gentlemen-huishers: then I pray you what number of chief mourners, of Lords, Knights, and Gentlemen, necessary, with their charges, and how many servants for them, besides my own preacher, physitian, lawyers; and XI cloaks for my own men; then LXIII women widows, the charges of the hearse, heralds, and church. Good Mr. Garter, do it exactly; for I find forewarnings that bid me provide a pick-axe, etc.: so with my most friendly commendations to you, I rest

Your old mistress, and friend,

ELIZABETH RUSSELL,

Dowager."[1]

Garter King of Arms took the letter in the spirit in which it was meant and replied in all solemnity, detailing that the chief mourner might have eleven yards of

[1] *A Complete Body of Heraldry*, J. Edmondson, vol. i.

material for her gown, the gentlewomen, four yards apiece, whilst every Earl's daughter attending, ten yards for her gown, mantle, train, hood, and tippets. Lady Russell did not die for many years to come, but it was a weight off her mind to be assured that if she did not become the wife of an earl, either with or without his full complement of wits, she would at least go to her own funeral as a viscountess.

In the meantime she erected a handsome monument in Bisham Church with an effigy of herself (a viscountess's coronet on her head) kneeling at prayer, surrounded by her dutiful family in pious imitation, and the Latin inscription (repeated also in Greek), composed by herself: *"Nemo Me Lachrymis Decoret, Neque Funera Fletio! Faxit cur! Vado Per Astra Deo!"*

LADY RUSSELL'S MONUMENT IN BISHAM CHURCH, NEAR GREAT MARLOW
Reproduced by the kind permission of the Walpole Society.

CHAPTER III

LADY RUSSELL'S family was more docile in effigy than in life, for the two sons of her first husband, and the elder at least of the two daughters by her second, had all inherited so much of their mother's temperament that their wills were in constant conflict with hers. Sir Edward Hoby, the eldest son, succeeded to his father's estates at Bisham; Elizabeth and Ann Russell were at Court as Maids of Honour to Queen Elizabeth, so the only one remaining with his mother was her younger son, Thomas Posthumus Hoby, so called because he was born after his father's death.

Lady Russell decided to make him a lawyer, and entered his name as a student at the Inns of Court. The wishes of Thomas Posthumus were not consulted at all in the matter, but though so undersized that he had been "reputed a child," he dared to oppose his will to his mother, and said flatly that he would not be a lawyer. Scarcely able to credit the evidence of her own ears, she asked what he did want to do, being further incensed when her insubordinate son replied he wished to go abroad. Lady Russell's opinion of "yong men's travell now a days" was that it resulted in "nothing but pryde, change, and vanytie in demming better of theyr own conceyts." It was useless for friends to tell her that "Home-keeping youth have ever homely wits," or to wonder that her ladyship

> "Would suffer him to spend his youth at home,
> While other men, of slender reputation,
> Put forth their sons to seek preferment out:
> Some to the wars, to try their fortune there;
> Some to discover islands far away;
> Some to the studious universities.
> For any or for all these exercises
> He said that Proteus your son was meet,
> And did request me to importune you
> To let him spend his time no more at home,
> Which would be great impeachment to his age,
> In having known no travel in his youth."[1]

Lord Burghley, whose opinion Lady Russell valued more than any one else's, upheld her opinion, saying, "Suffer not thy sons to pass the Alps, for they shall learn nothing there but pride, blasphemy, and atheism." Instead of becoming proficient in foreign languages, which was the ostensible reason for their travels, they returned wearing strange clothes, swore still stranger oaths, were unsettled in religion, and of such good opinion of themselves that they opposed their wills to their lady mother's. Thomas Posthumus was quite troublesome enough as it was without running any risk of his fulfilling the current saying, "An Italianized Englishman is a devil

---

[1] *The Two Gentlemen of Verona*, I, 3.

incarnate." He should stop at home, mind his book, and become a lawyer.

The affectations of travelled young men had become such a joke that Elizabeth and Ann Russell and the rest of the Maids of Honour would flout them saying:

"Farewell, Monsieur Traveller: Look you lisp, and wear strange suits; disable all the benefits of your own country; be out of love with your nativity, and almost chide God for making you that countenance you are; or I will scarce think you have swam in a gondola."[1]

As Lady Russell persisted in her determination to carry out her plan despite her son's emphatic "refusall to take that course of law which might i' end bredd to my comfort and his owne good," he formed the desperate resolve of running away to sea. Lady Russell, following hard on his heels, overtook the fugitive in the Isle of Sheppey and brought him back captive to her house in the Blackfriars. For several days a virtuously indignant mother treated her sullenly obstinate son with frigid politeness in public, not wishing to reveal to servants the "war between myne own flesh and blood"; but in private she did not scruple to let him know, "what his owne infirmityes and insufficiency by want of stature, learning, and otherwise be."

At her wit's end to know what to do, Lady Russell wrote to her brother-in-law, Lord Burghley, concerning "the unnaturall hard nature and insolency of this boy," who defied her authority: " though my naturall

[1] *As You Like It*, iv, i.

inclinacion have ben, by love and reason to procure my children to love, and feare me ; yet I have not deserved thereby contempt, nor shewed myself simple, in being ignorant of my due, and valew of my desart."

Lord Burghley, though he disliked being waited on by kinsmen, came to his sister-in-law's assistance and agreed to take young Hoby into his household for the time being. When Lady Russell's anger had somewhat abated, she came to the conclusion that, as nothing would induce Thomas Posthumus to become a lawyer, the only alternative career would be as the husband of an heiress. For once the unruly youth proved compliant; he infinitely preferred an heiress to the law. Lady Russell in high good humour promised that in the event of such a marriage she would make him a good allowance, always provided he proved a biddable son and allowed her to choose her own daughter-in-law.

Soon after mother and son had come to this amicable agreement, news reached London of the death in France of the Earl of Essex's brother, Walter Devereux, "that diamond of the time, both of a hardy and delicate temper and mixture."[1] Lady Russell's thoughts at once flew to the widow, Margaret, daughter and heiress of Mr. Dakins of Hackness in Yorkshire; young, rich, and of sound religious principles; here was the very wife for Thomas Posthumus.

Lady Russell lost no time, but going to Lord Burghley's house in the Strand she entreated him to use his influence in the matter. As Walter Devereux had not

[1] *Reliquiæ Wottonianæ.*

been dead a fortnight, the Lord High Treasurer was averse to moving in the matter quite so soon, but his sister-in-law overruled his scruples by representing that there was no time like the present. So rich a young widow would doubtless have many suitors, and in the interests of Thomas Posthumus his uncle must act at once.

In the end, Lady Russell carried the day, and Lord Burghley promised to write both to the lady's father and to the Earl of Huntingdon,[1] who as Walter Devereux's guardian would expect to be consulted about the widow's remarriage. To the Earl of Huntingdon Lord Burghley wrote first:

"My very good Lord: The harty love and dutyfull goodwyll that I knowe to be borne your Lp: by my good La: and syster the La: Russell, maketh me bowlde to joyne with her, as a mother for hir sonne, and myself for my honest servante and nephewe to commend to your Lps: favore his intentions to seeke, by your Lps: both meanes and advyce, to be a suter to a late yonge widdowe that was wyfe to Mr. Walter Devereux. And if your Lp: shall please to give my La: comforte therin, I wyll joyne with hyr in prosecution therof both to the wyddowe, and any other her freynds she may be advysed by. And I doubt not but the yonge gentlemane, though he be Posthumus by his father's death, beyng born after, yet my La: hath such respect to hym, and he soe well doth and wyll deserve yt, as he shall be able to be a father of lyvehode. And I can

1 Henry Hastings, 3rd Earl Huntingdon.

assure you Lp: by the proofe that I have had at his good nature and conditions, he wyll prove a good and corteous husbande, and a keeper and noe spender. And soe wyshynge to heer of your Lps: good recovery,

Your Lps: most assuredly to comm:"[1]

As it happened, this letter proved a fatal mistake, for it gave the Earl of Huntingdon warning that there was another suitor in the field, whereas he had made up his mind that Margaret should marry his wife's[2] favourite nephew, Thomas Sidney.[3]

The Huntingdons, a childless couple themselves, had all the anxieties of a large family, for not only had Margaret Dakins been brought up by them, but the Earl was also guardian to the four handsome, wayward Devereux[4] boys and girls, whose high spirits gave their guardian a world of trouble. Robert, Earl of Essex, despite his youth, had carried all before him at Court, and was now the Queen's chief favourite; Walter, who had married the heiress of Hackness and led a rollicking life with the squires of the Yorkshire dales, had died a soldier's death before Rouen. The girls, Penelope and Dorothy, inherited the beauty of their mother, Lettice Knollys, who in her youth when Maid of Honour had

[1] *The Fortescue Papers* (Camden Society).
[2] Catherine, d. of John Dudley, Duke of Northumberland.
[3] Son of Sir Henry Sidney (1529–1586) and his wife, Mary Dudley, sister of Lady Huntingdon and the Earl of Leicester.
[4] Children of Walter Devereux, 1st Earl of Essex (d. 1576), and his wife, Lettice, d. of Sir Francis Knollys.

wrested the Earl of Leicester's affection from the Queen. Penelope's father had wished her to marry Sir Philip Sidney, but the Earl of Huntingdon sought a more wealthy husband for his beautiful fourteen-year-old ward in the person of "the rich Lord Rich,"[1] Dorothy, the younger girl, did not trouble to consult her guardian at all, for she made a runaway marriage with Sir Thomas Perrot,[2] which had got every one concerned into disgrace with the Queen.

The Huntingdons were determined not to run any risks in the present instance, so, when they learnt that Mr. Thomas Posthumus Hoby wanted to pay court to Walter Devereux's widow, they sent Thomas Sidney off in all speed to Yorkshire, requesting that the heiress should be sent down to them in London immediately.

Therefore it happened that when Mr. Dakins received a letter from Lord Burghley, offering his nephew as a son-in-law, he was not a little perturbed at having to reply: "the which to answer as I woolde I noe ways can, which breedeth some griefe in me for that my daughter toke her jorney the 2 of this instant November laste with my lettres to the Right Honorable therle of Huntyndon, and the Countess his wyfe, her owlde mistress; yeeldynge therby my consente to theyr honors for the disposynge of my daughter in her maryadge, which God knoweth is meane, and fair unworthy the proffer your Ho: doth make by your sayde letteres."[3] ·

[1] Robert Rich, 1st Earl of Warwick.
[2] Son of Sir John Perrot, reputed son of Henry VIII.
[3] *The Fortescue Papers.*

When Lady Russell and her son realized that the Huntingdons had other plans for the heiress they were extremely vexed, but by no means disheartened. The first thing to do was to find out if the lady really was in London, for the Huntingdons were keeping it very dark, and no one knew for certain if she had arrived.

Lady Russell endeavoured to enlist the support of the Earl of Essex, but he was annoyed with his sister-in-law for being in such a hurry to remarry, and would do nothing. Dorothy Perrot proved more amenable, and promised to try and find out if Margaret really was in town; if so, she would invite her on a visit, and then Mr. Hoby should see her.

Lady Perrot did her best, but it did not amount to much, and she wrote to tell the anxious Thomas Posthumus the meagre result of her endeavours:

"Mr. Hoby; I sent a man of myne who long served her to my Lady of Huntingdon from me, who as of him selfe did inquier of the gentill woman you knowe of; but could learne nothing of her coming up. If you will have me send to knowe as from myselfe, I will, or what else I may do your liking; I pray you remember me humbly to my Lady, and so I leave you to all good happys, this first day of November.

Your frend that wisheth you well,

D. PERROT."

A little later Lady Perrot was able to inform the anxious suitor that "the gentillwoman you knowe of is

come to my Lord of Huntingdon's." It was very difficult
to get information, for the Huntingdons were on their
guard, and as soon as Margaret arrived in town she was
taken up to her room, "which she closely kept untyll
she was maryed." Visitors were not encouraged, Margaret being a "prysoner in her chamber, whyther none
were suffered to come, without especiall admyttance."
Among the favoured few was Thomas Sidney, "but not
as a suitor till the funeral is past."

The Huntingdons would have married the young
people at once had it not been that Walter Devereux's
body still remained in France, and etiquette forbade the
widow to remarry till after her husband's burial.

In this delay lay Lady Russell's hope. Thomas
Posthumus had indeed lost heart, but his mother was of
tougher metal, and had she been a man would never
have allowed a destined bride to be given to a rival.
There were other ways of winning a lady than by knock-
ing at the front door and asking her guardian's consent.
Anthony Cooke,[1] her nephew, was a venturesome young
man; let him and Posthumus put their heads together
and concoct a plan to abduct Mistress Devereux. Lady
Russell sat down and wrote to her son:

"Posthumus. I have sent you what I have rec(eived).
Shew Mr. Stanley's letter to me unto my Lord and
Master. Now chyld, it standeth you aper for your owne
creditt's sake to trye your freends. My La: Perrott
the wisest, surest, fittest to your good, who, after she

[1] Son of Richard, eldest son of Sir A. Cooke.

31

hath found her disposityon touching Sidney, may, on some tyme of the gentlewoman's comming to visitt my La: Dorothie, let you understand of the tyme when yourself may mete her there. Yf this prove a matche, I will be bound to leave to you that which shall be worth V.C. LI. by yere, wherof III.C. LI. of it joynter to her after my death, and a house presently furnished to bring her to. Yf in affeċtion she be gon to Sidney, it is one thing: if by reason she be willing to be ledd to her owne good, you will be found the better mache of bothe.

"I have promised your brother to depay the charge of assurances for the entayle of Bisham, which I consent to for fear of sayle. He sayth it will cost me 40 li. I pray God it be worth so much to yourself.

Your most loving mother,
ELIZABETH RUSSELL.

I would you coold so use the matter that the widdow be here this Christmas. I have appoynted your brother's mustyons: have hard them and given the master v.s. earnest. Let Anthony Cooke help to steale her away. She hath her father's consent to match where she lists."

It was no use, for the heiress had fallen in love with Thomas Sidney, and married him as soon as she decently could. Three years later, in 1595, Margaret, now owner of Hackness in her own right, was a widow again. Young Hoby, who in the interval had been knighted, lost no time at all in renewing his suit. Unfortunately he was not at the moment on good terms with his mother; on very bad ones, indeed, for he had run away to sea in good earnest, and she had refused even to see him since his return from abroad.

It was very embarrassing for Sir Thomas Posthumus, because being in mortal terror of her ladyship he was afraid to accept any invitations where there was any likelihood of Lady Russell being present. The newly made Knight dare not even attend the Court festivities, "which in respect of my mother I could not, which grieved me not a little, I protest. But not being admitted to see my mother since my last return into England, if I should the first time have seen her in so public an assembly, either I must have made them all privy to her unkind strangeness, by offering to do my duty which would have been offensive to her, or else I must have omitted that which I am bound to perform, which God willing, shall never be found in me."[1]

All the same, Posthumus saw little chance of success in his wooing unless Lady Russell did support him, for he was entirely dependent on her, and had nothing on his own account to offer his prospective bride "but my virtue which is wonderful and rare." Not daring to approach his indignant parent himself, he took a roundabout course, writing to Sir Robert Cecil to ask him to get Lord Burghley to speak to Lady Russell, as he finds "his lady mother so backward for his preferment that

[1] Hatfield MS. v.

he has no other hope to draw her to do anything but by the Lord Treasurer's means."

Through Lord Burghley's mediation Lady Russell and her son were once more reconciled, and together prosecuted an eager pursuit of the Yorkshire heiress. The lady was still at Hackness, for though she and Hoby had heard a great deal of one another they had never met, and on the gentleman's side the anxiety to do so was very keen. He besought his friends to write letters of commendation on his behalf to the Earl and Countess of Huntingdon, who now they had no nephew of their own to put forward might be disposed to look more favourably on himself. So indeed it proved, and the Earl of Huntingdon appointed Mr. Stanhope, one of his gentlemen, to escort the ardent suitor north, where he might have an interview with Mistress Margaret Sidney, who was staying at Hull.

It was one o'clock when the two men arrived at the Manor, and Mr. Stanhope was ushered into a room where he found the lady lying on a couch, and complaining of pain in her eyes, occasioned by the tears she had shed for the "worthy gentleman her late husband." Indeed as soon as Mr. Stanhope began to offer condolences the widow began to cry again, which was extremely disconcerting for him, knowing that the letter he carried in his hand from the Earl of Huntingdon was to suggest a new husband, who, moreover, waited impatiently in another room.

Mistress Margaret read the letter whilst the tears ran down her cheeks, for she said that though she felt

34

herself in duty bound to attend her guardian's wishes, "yet the tender love she bare to him that was dead, made yt grevous to hear of any newe, and much more to be thought of the gentleman that she were to be delt with any such matter soe soone."

Stanhope hastened to say that Sir Thomas Hoby had foreseen this objection, and "had that revered regard of her, in that in his owne opinione he might be thought to blame; but that two respects ledd him. One, is desire his eyes to witnes that which publick report had delivered him, that the guyftes of nature had in some sort equalled her vertues. Thother, having bene longe draune to affect her for thes guyftes he was desirous to be made knowne to her, as the first that shoulde seeke her, though he after forbore for some tyme to entertayne or present his suyte."[1]

Mr. Stanhope tactfully persuaded, till at length he won the lady to say that, as it was the Earl of Huntingdon's desire, she would see Sir Thomas, as she did not wish to appear discourteous to "a gentleman of his worth that came so far for that purpose."

Mr. Stanhope took the good news back to Posthumus, but he had to wait another half-hour whilst Mistress Margaret changed her dress, bathed her eyes, and made herself ready for company. Unfortunately, when Sir Thomas Posthumus at length saw the lady he had wooed so long unknown, he was tongue-tied with shyness. Luckily Mr. Stanhope rose to the occasion, and made all the conventional pretty speeches in his friend's name,

[1] *The Fortescue Papers.*

which Sir Thomas himself would have said if he had not been too bashful to say anything but monosyllables.

The heiress created a very favourable impression on Sir Thomas, so that he announced his intention of letting the lady know "that he was so fully satisfied by sight of her, that all things answerable to the good reporte he had recyved of her before, as he ment to settle himself in her favor." In the meantime he returned to London to report good progress to his mother, who was so pleased that she supplied him "with a good store of faire jewels and pearls," to take as a present to her prospective daughter-in-law.

Neither mother nor son anticipated for one moment that the heiress could be other than delighted at the prospect of marrying Sir Thomas Posthumus Hoby. As a matter of fact, she was nothing of the sort; after being matched to a handsome Devereux, and a cultured Sidney, she had no mind to a little undersized Knight who couldn't say bo to a goose, much less make love to a lady. She gave the servants orders not to admit Sir Thomas next time he called, and wrote off to her guardian flatly refusing to have anything whatever to do with the suitor he had commended to her.

The Earl of Huntingdon, in ill-health, and bombarded with letters from Hoby's powerful relations, and as a last straw, by the importunate young man himself, requiring explanation why the door of Hull Manor had been shut in his face, wrote to his ward in reply:

"Mrs. Margaret,

"Beare with me whatsoever I wryte, for I was not in a greater payne synce my last jorney than I even nowe ame in. I did acquaynte hym with the contents of your lettre, and at the laste I dyd geve hym the lettre to peruse, but yt moved him not to that purpose you desyred. And soe he toulde me he woolde tell yourself, yet withoute my lettre he woolde not returne. He doth not believe that you will geve such denyall as your lettre mentioneth. For God's cause have care of all your credyts, and soe handle the matter at his commynge agayne may be neyther offensyve to you nor dyspleasynge to himself. And so with wysh of all good and happynes to you for this tyme I ende and commyt you to the L. Jesus. At York this 9th Dec:

Your lovynge freynde,

H. HUNTYNGDON."

This letter was one of the last the Earl wrote, for his illness took a serious turn, and five days later he died. The persevering Sir Thomas, who still refused to take the heiress's emphatic "no" for an answer, endeavoured to get the widowed Countess of Huntingdon on his side. She was too heartbroken to trouble about the matter which concerned her so little, for Margaret, at the age of twenty-four having had two husbands, was surely competent to choose a third one for herself. Since Sir Thomas Hoby had her late husband's approbation she would not be against him; since Margaret disliked him she would not be for him.

Hoby next tried the relatives of the heiress's previous husbands, hoping they might have sufficient influence with the young widow to make her sensible of the new suitor's manifold merits to which she remained so woefully indifferent. Sir Robert Sidney promised to do what he could with his sister-in-law, but the Earl of Essex, still annoyed at Margaret's hasty second marriage, would not concern himself at all with her third. His wife, to whom Hoby also wrote, replied in much the same strain as Lady Huntingdon, but gave warning of a rival:

"Sir,

"I have receaved your letter, the contentes wherof being honest and honorably, doe so fullie free you, in my conceit, from all imputation of presumption, as that I would willinglie have testified both my approbation and furderance of the matter to your M^{res} if I had not of late beene much importuned to writte in the same argument by some that persuaded themselves I had small reason (besides my will) to denie them (as they thought) so reasonable a request, and if I would have been an achtor in marige mattars, I would not have refust them my fourdrans. Let thes excus my not sattesfieing your request, not but that I holde you worthe of har you desir, but that in honnor I cannot be for you sens I have promest an othar not to be aganst him. I comitt you to the protection of the Higheyst.

Your loving frend,

F^r. Essex."

38

Margaret was indeed free to marry where she liked, and her choice would certainly not have fallen on Thomas Posthumus, had not the new Earl of Huntingdon, on looking through his brother's papers, conceived himself the real owner of Hackness, on the plea that the Earl of Huntingdon had provided part of Margaret Dakins's dowry. Faced with a lawsuit and possible loss of her property, the widow listened to the one indisputable asset in Hoby's favour, namely, that he was the nephew of the powerful Lord Burghley: it would be very much better to have the Lord High Treasurer for her than against her. Margaret thought the matter over and accepted Thomas Posthumus.

Overjoyed at his good fortune, the prospective bridegroom wrote to invite his cousin, Anthony Bacon, to the wedding feast, which was to take place at Lady Russell's house in the Blackfriars, on August 9th, 1596, "when," said Posthumus, "I seeke only to please the beholders with a sermon and a dinner, and myself with beholding my mistress."

Lady Russell, in high good humour, conveyed the glad news to her nephew, Sir Robert Cecil:

"Mr. Secretary,
"My son, God willing, is to be married on Monday, being the 9th of August, here at my house in the Blackfriars. My meaning is not to make any solemnity, but only a private meeting of good and honourable friends, a few. Whereof (if it please you and my lady, your wife, to be chief) as friends to my son and fairest

flower of his garland for friendship when I am gone, is all my desire at this time. I mean to send my coach for my two daughters, and appoint them whom they shall bring with them, whereof Sir Robert Sidney and Sir William Brook to be two against that time. So loth to trouble you longer from your affairs at this time I take my leave. From my house at the Blackfriars, this first of August,

Your unfortunate Aunt,

ELIZABETH RUSSELL, Dowager."

CHAPTER IV

AFTER the wedding, the Hobys went north to Hackness, there "to keep hospitality and lead ordinary country life." Margaret, fully occupied with the cares of a large household and estate, kept a diary wherein she chronicled the small happenings which made her days so full. Mistress and maids dyed wool, wound yarn, made wax lights, sweetmeats, gingerbread, and in summer were busy with their preserving pans. Long winter evenings found them seated at spinning-wheels and embroidery frames, whilst one of their number read aloud some devotional book.

In everything connected with her inheritance Margaret Hoby took an active interest. Riding over the estate she supervised haymaking, overlooked the buying of sheep, kept a watchful eye on the crops, and paid the workmen their wages. The tenants came to her when they were ill, and she doctored them with medicine of her own compounding. Caring little for the active field sports of hunting or falconry wherein Queen Elizabeth and most ladies of the time delighted, Margaret's favourite amusements were fishing and bowls. Part of each day was devoted to reading the Bible and writing out sermons or spiritual exercises under the guidance of the domestic chaplain.

As a country gentleman, Sir Thomas Posthumus was less successful, for in truth the part fitted him very ill. The jovial sportsmen of the Yorkshire dales drank deep and swore hard, "abuses never practised by Sir Thomas"; whilst their conversation related chiefly to the doings of horse and hound, "sports whereunto Sir Thomas never applied himself."

As Sir Thomas showed such lamentable lack of good fellowship, and was, moreover, so inclined to be quarrelsome, they ridiculed him as "the little Knight that useth to draw up his breeches with a shooing-horn,"[1] and reckoned him "one of the cross accidents of life."[2]

One reason for his unpopularity arose from the fact that he was a Puritan, one of those cold-blooded men who would sing "psalms to horn-pipes,"[3] and wanted to put down the "sweet and comfortable" sport of bear-baiting; not because it gave pain to the bear, but because it gave pleasure to the spectator. The country gentlemen who, in rare moments of reflection, would say, "I would I had bestowed that time in the tongues that I have in fencing, dancing, and bear-baiting,"[4]

---

[1] James Howell's *Familiar Letters*.
[2] *Memoirs of Sir Hugh Cholmley*.
[3] *The Winter's Tale*, iv, 2.
[4] *Twelfth Night*, i, 3.

were highly indignant at the very suggestion. Because
a Puritan went about,

> "With purpose to be dress'd in an opinion
> Of wisdom, gravity, profound conceit,
> As who should say 'I am Sir Oracle,
> And when I ope my lips let no dog bark!' "[1]

it by no means followed that other folk were of the
same opinion. "Dost thou think, because thou art
virtuous, there shall be no more cakes and ale?" asked
the sport-loving squires, aroused to wrath by the very
name of Puritan. One convivial party of boon companions who came to Hackness uninvited after a day's
hunting, were greatly incensed at the lack of hospitality,
and drink, offered to them. Especially they resented their
host's refusal to play cards or drink healths, "contrary
to his disposition,"[2] wherefore they called Sir Thomas
Posthumus "a scurvy urchen" and "a spindle-shanked
ape"; moreover, they threatened "to play young
Devereux" with him, and to "pull him by the beard"
next time they met him, yea, even if he should be on
the Justices' bench.

Lady Hoby staunchly upheld her lord in his quarrels,
for though she had been so very unwilling to take him
for a third husband, the marriage proved a suitable one,
for Margaret's strong Puritan tendencies received every
consideration and encouragement at his hands. With

[1] *The Merchant of Venice*, I, I.
[2] For further particulars of this quarrel see Appendix,
"Shakespeare and a Yorkshire Quarrel," p. 238.

no children to occupy her thoughts, religion became the abiding interest in Lady Hoby's life, and she looked forward to visiting London, chiefly for the opportunity of hearing the most celebrated preachers of the day. Her favourite pastor was Mr. Stephen Egerton,[1] a famous Puritan divine "of great learning and godliness," who held daily and weekly lectures at Lady Russell's Parish Church, St. Anne's, Blackfriars, "a little Church or Chappel up stayres, but a great congregation especially of women." Many times did Lady Hoby enter in her diary:

"I went to Mr. Egerton's sermon and after came to my Lady Russell's to dinner; after I went againe to his exercise and thence home to my lodgings."[2]

Other clergy, jealous of Mr. Egerton's popularity, complained "many of their parishioners leaving their own pastors and flocking to Mr. Egerton," and openly "reprehended Mr. Egerton, and such as other popular preachers, that their auditory being most of women abounded in superfluous apparaile."[3]

Even unpopular clergymen had fairly good congregations on Sundays, since the Act of 1593 enacted that every one over sixteen must go to church "or in default

[1] Stephen Egerton, Puritan divine; suspended for refusing to subscribe to Whitgift's Articles, 1584; imprisoned 1590; introduced petition to the lower house of Convocation for a reformed Prayer Book, 1604.

[2] Egerton MS. 2614. British Museum.

[3] Manningham's *Diary* (Camden Society).

44

to be hanged or banished." After all, even a dull sermon was preferable to being hanged, though the thoughts of the male members of the congregation often strayed anxiously towards their Sunday dinners. One minister, asking a gentleman his opinion of the sermon, received the sulky reply, "'Twas very good, but that it had spoyled a goose worth two of it."[1]

After making outward observance of their faith at morning prayer congregations might do as they pleased for the rest of the day.

"Now when dinner once is done, and that they well have fed,
To play they go, to casting of the stone, to runne, or shoote;
To tosse the light and windy ball aloft with hand or foot,
Some others to trie their skill in gonnes; some wastrell all the
   day;
And some to schooles of fence do goe, to gaze upon the
   play;
Another sort there is, that doth not love abroad to roame,
But, for to pass their time at cards, or tables,[2] still at home."[3]

If wives accused their husbands of thinking more of dinner and games than the sermon, they rounded on the ladies by accusing them of going to church to show off their clothes, or get ideas for new ones.

"What though she rideth ten miles on holy days
To church, as others do to feasts and plays,
To shew their tires, to view and to be viewed."[4]

---

[1] Thoms's *Anecdotes and Traditions.*
[2] Backgammon.
[3] Strutt's *Sports and Pastimes.*
[4] Ben Jonson's *Underwoods.*

Ballad singers too sang of a heartless spouse who denied his wife's reasonable request:

> "Nay t'other day at church I spide a hat
> My mind and eye was never off from that,
> The only fashion to content alone,
> Yet think you he would buy me such a one
> No, I protest, but when I made the motion,
> Oh wife (said he) pray where was your devotion?
> Go you to church to find new fashions out?
> Is this the exercise you are about?"[1]

Whatever their motives the feminine portion of the congregation were manifestly at a disadvantage when the clergyman chose to direct his eloquence against them. It was a subject that even the youngest preacher essayed without diffidence. One Sunday at St. Paul's Cross a boyish parson made a "finicall boysterous" sermon, "against pride in beauty, the devil plays the sophister while he persuades women to paint that they may seeme fayrer than they are; which painting being discovered, make them to be thought fouler than they are. Pride in apparell is pride of our shame, for it was made to cover it." The presumptuous young man must have felt the profound silence with which the ladies, tricked out in their Sunday best, listened to this tirade, for he grew so nervous that his subject got out of hand and he "ran himself at almost dry before he was halfe through his text."[2]

Even Queen Elizabeth, who possessed three thousand

[1] *A Whole Crew of Kind Gossips*, S. Rowlands.
[2] Manningham's *Diary*.

PREACHING AT ST. PAUL'S CROSS.
Reproduced by the kind permission of " Society of Antiquaries of London."

gowns of inconceivable richness, and eighty wigs of variable hues, once heard some plain speaking on the vanity of dress : but in this instance the congregation was in a position to defend itself, and it did so.

"One Sunday (April last) my lord of London preached to the Queen's Majesty; and seemed to touch on the vanity of decking the body too finely. Her Majesty told the ladies, that if the bishop held more discourse on such matters, she would fit him for heaven; but he should walk thither without a staff, and leave his mantle behind him. Perchance the bishop hath never sought her highness' wardrobe, or he would have chosen another text."[1]

Authority had done its unsuccessful best to cope with feminine extravagance, and failed. The County of Surrey even attempted to judge a man's income by the richness of his wife's dress, ordaining, "If any person be thought of ability to be charged by reason of lands or goods, or by their *wives apparell*, they are to be so charged." It would have been more reasonable to deduce a corresponding reduction of his household goods commensurate with his wife's finery:

"'Roome! Roome!' said one, 'here comes a woman with a cupboard on hir head,' of one that had sold hir cupboard to buy a taffety hat."[2]

It was all very well for an unmarried parson to get up

[1] *Nugæ Antiquæ*, Sir John Harington.
[2] Manningham's *Diary*.

In the pulpit and cry out "against the excessive pride
and vanitie of women in apparaile, etc: which vice he
said was in their husband's power to correct." Husbands
could only shrug their shoulders and say, "Then she
plots, then she ruminates, then she devises; and what
they think in their hearts they may effect, they will
break their hearts, but they will effect."[1]

The extravagance and vagaries of the opposite sex
was a favourite topic with elderly gentlemen. Many a
maiden could tell of "an old religious uncle," who
railed against *Woman,* till his hearers said, "I thank
God I am not a woman, to be touched with so many
giddy offences as he hath generall taxed their whole
sex withal." A curious man might ask, "Can you remember any of the principal evils that he laid to the
charge of women?" Only to be told, "There were
none principal; they were all like one another as half-
pence are; every one fault seeming monstrous till his
fellow fault came to match it."[2]

The extravagance of ·women! the money they spend
on clothes! Well might husbands exclaim:

"To furnishe a shipp requireth much trouble
But to furnishe a woman the charges are double."

Women and the Stage—those were the two crying
evils of the time according to the clergy, the Puritans,
and would-be social reformers. "Wyll not a fylthye
playe wyth the blast of a trumpette sooner call thyther

[1] *The Merry Wives of Windsor,* II, 2.
[2] *As You Like It,* III, 2.

48

a thousande than an houres tolling of a bell bring to the sermon a hundred?"[1] The answer was in the affirmative; therein lay the sting. It was no use telling the public:

"Playes are the inventions of the devil, the offrings of Idolatrie, the pompe of worldlings, the blossomes of vanitie, the roote of Apostacy, the foode of iniquitie, regret, and adulterie, detest them. Players are masters of vice, teachers of wantonnesse, spurres to impuritie, the sonnes of idlenesse, so longe as they live in this order, loathe them."[2]

The public did nothing of the sort; it made idols of popular actors, and continued to imperil the safety of its soul for the gratification of seeing Mr. William Shakespeare's plays performed at "The Theatre," the famous playing-house in the fields at Shoreditch. The lease of "The Theatre" expired in 1597, and, as there was difficulty about renewing it, James Burbage, the proprietor, bought a house in the Blackfriars and proceeded to convert it into a playhouse.

Residents and the Puritan colony at Blackfriars made great outcry at the prospect, for the proposed theatre would transform their peaceful neighbourhood, filling the narrow streets with noisy crowds entirely objectionable to the quiet folk who lived among the ruins of the old priory.[3] The most energetic opponent to the plan

[1] John Stockwood's Sermon, 1578.

[2] *Playes Confuted in Five Actions*, Stephen Gosson.

[3] Blackfriars Priory surrendered to King Henry VIII on Nov. 12th, 1538. Catherine of Aragon's trial took place there in 1529.

was Lady Russell, who got up a petition to be presented to the Lords of the Council, which she and thirty other residents in the precincts of the Blackfriars signed, amongst them being Lord Hunsdon,[1] who was patron of the theatrical company, but wanted to buy the house himself; Stephen Egerton, the minister of St. Anne's; Dr. William Paddy,[2] the famous physician; Ascanius de Renialme, a bookseller; and Richard Field,[3] the printer.

PETITION OF THE INHABITANTS OF THE BLACKFRIARS[4]

"To the Right Honble. the Lords and others of her Majesties most honorable Privy Councell, 1596.

"Humbly shewing and beseeching your honors, the inhabitants of the precinct of the Blackfryers London,

[1] George Carey, 2nd Lord Hunsdon, m. Elizabeth Spencer, d. of Sir J. Spencer of Althorp. He succeeded his father 1596 and gave his patronage to his father's company of players. 1597 Lord Hunsdon was appointed Lord Chamberlain, and his company of players were known as the Lord Chamberlain's men. Shakespeare belonged to this company and his plays were produced by it.

[2] Sir William Paddy, physician to James I. Knighted 1603; President of the College of Physicians, 1609, 1610, 1611, and 1618; benefactor to St. John's College, Oxford, where he is buried.

[3] Richard Field of Stratford-on-Avon; Master Stationers' Company, 1620. Printed Shakespeare's *Venus and Adonis*, 1593, and first edition of *Lucrece*, 1594.

[4] Dom. State Papers. Eliz.

That whereas one Burbage has lately bought certaine roomes in the same precinct neere adjoyning unto the dwelling-houses of the Rt. Honorable the Lord Chamberlain and the Lord of Hunsdon, which roomes the said Burbage is now altering and meaneth very shortly to convert and turn the same into a common playhouse which will grow to be a very great annoyance and trouble, not only to all the noblemen and gentlemen thereabout inhabiting, but allso a generall inconvenience to all the inhabitants of the same Precinct both by reason of the great resort and gathering together of vagrant and leude persons, that under cullor of resorting to the Playes will come thither and worke all manner of mischeefe and allso to the greate pestering and filling up of the same precinct, yf it should please God to send any visitation of sicknesse as heretofore hath been, for that the same Playhouse is so neere the Church that the noyse of the Drumms and Trumpets will greatly disturbe and hinder both the Ministers and parishioners in tyme of devine service and sermons. In tender consideracion whereof As allso for that there hath not at any tyme heretofore been used any comon Playhouse within the same Precinct But that now all Players being banished by the Lord Mayor from playing within the Cittie, by reason of the great inconveniences and ill rule that followeth them they now thinke to plant themselves in liberties. That therefore it would please your honors to take order that the same Roomes may be converted to some other use and that no Playhouse may be used or kept there. And your suppliants as most bounden shall and will dayly pray for your Lordships in all honor and happiness long to live."

Lady Russell presented her petition to the Privy Council during November 1596, and it was successful in so much that in deference to the desires of the Blackfriars residents the opening of a public playhouse[1] in their midst was prohibited. A theatre of sorts, though, it still remained, albeit a private one, being leased to the Master of "The Children of the Chapel Royal." Ostensibly Choristers, these were clever little mimics, whose theatrical performances so seriously rivalled the adult companies as to occasion a reference in Hamlet.

"But there is, Sir, an aery of children, little eyases,[2] that cry out on the top of question, and are most tyrannically clapped for 't: these are now the fashion, and so berattle the common stages,—so they call them, —that many wearing rapiers are afraid of goose quills and dare scarce come thither."[3]

[1] It was not till after Lady Russell's death in 1609 that the Blackfriars theatre was opened as a public playhouse, Shakespeare being one of the shareholders.

[2] Eyas = a young hawk imperfectly trained for falconry.

[3] *Hamlet*, II, 2.

CHAPTER V

THEATRICAL controversies held little interest for Lady Hoby's sister-in-law, Barbara,[1] wife of Sir Robert Sidney,[2] whose life was bound up in husband, home, and children. In her youth she too had been an heiress with many suitors at her feet, but when the second of the three famous Sidney brothers came to woo, he won the Welsh heiress as his brother Thomas did the Yorkshire one. Thereby he incurred the displeasure of Her Majesty, Queen Elizabeth, who had other views for the young heiress, and sent messengers off post-haste to forbid her marriage with Sir Robert Sidney. These arrived too late to cross the path of true love, for Barbara Gamage had already become Lady Sidney when she received the royal prohibition.

The marriage proved a very happy one, and the young couple settled down to keep open house at their family place, Penshurst, in Kent.

[1] D. of John Gamage of Coytie, Glamorganshire. She married Sir Robert Sidney in 1584. Their family consisted of two sons and eight daughters.

[2] Second son of Sir H. Sidney, created Viscount Lisle, 1605; Earl of Leicester, 1618.

> "And though thy walls be of the country stone,
> They're reared with no man's ruin, no man's groan;
> There's none that dwell about them wish them down;
> But all come in, the farmer and the clown."[1]

Barbara's housekeeping was famous, and the farms, meadows, river, fishponds, and orchard were laid under tribute to provide the good cheer for her hospitable table. "The painted partridge," and "the purpled pheasant with the speckled side," abounded in the fields and woods, whilst from the orchards came fruit:

> "The early cherry, with the later plum,
> Fig, grape, and quince, each in his time doth come:
> The blushing apricot, and woolly peach
> Hang on thy walls, that every child may reach."

Country folk who prided themselves on their home-made cheeses and cakes would bring them as presents to the kindly lady at Penshurst, who bade them all welcome and interested herself in their troubles and affairs. No one who came to Penshurst of whatsoever degree need fear the warmth of their welcome, for Lady Sidney's generous and kindly nature greeted all alike. Even poets, peculiarly sensitive about their social status, knew that at Penshurst they would be treated with due respect, and not placed at the lower end of the table or served with coarser viands than those provided for host and hostess. Such churlish hospitality

[1] *The Forest* (" To Penshurst "), Ben Jonson.

might be practised elsewhere, but not at Sir Robert and
Lady Sidney's:

"Whose liberal board doth flow,
With all that hospitality doth know!
Where comes no guest, but is allow'd to eat,
Without his fear, and of thy lord's own meat:
Where the same beer and bread, and self-same wine,
That is his lordship's, shall be also mine.
And I not fain to sit (as some this day,
At great men's tables) and yet dine away."

Barbara Sidney knew how to make her guests feel at
home, for she personally visited every bedroom to
make sure that fires and lights were in readiness, and
nothing lacking to ensure the visitors' complete comfort.
Touched and gratified by the care their hostess had
taken, guests would assure her, "There's nothing I can
wish, for which I stay," and that they felt as if they
were in their own homes.

Apart from household cares, Lady Sidney devoted a
great deal of time to her ever-increasing family of little
ones who romped about the grounds, or played hide-
and-seek round the oak tree which had been planted
at the birth of their famous uncle, Sir Philip Sidney.
Mother and children loved the dappled deer which
roamed the park, and a favourite amusement was to
take baskets of bread to "Gamage Copse," so called in
honour of Barbara, where the large-eyed animals would
crowd round to take food from the children's hands.
The little ones were too young for many lessons as yet,
but their watchful mother, knowing how much early

55

home influence would count in after life, taught them unaware the seeds of discipline and religion which should form the groundwork of their characters. Visitors never failed to notice the quiet, well-behaved children who were always present at morning and evening family prayers.

> "They are, and have been taught religion; thence
> Their gentler spirits have suck'd innocence.
> Each morn, and even, they are taught to pray,
> With the whole household, and may, every day,
> Read in their virtuous parents' noble parts,
> The mysteries of manners, arms, and arts."

The Sidneys would gladly have passed their days in their happy country home, but Queen Elizabeth appointed Sir Robert Governor of Flushing, which entailed long absences from his wife and family. Elizabeth, who knew a good man when she found one, placed such reliance on Sidney that she was very chary indeed of giving him leave of absence from his post.

Barbara, caring little for town life, would have remained at Penshurst with her children, but in order to use her own and her friends' influence for Sir Robert's recall she decided to go up to London in the autumn of 1595. She found it easier to come to the decision than to get a house, for the Sidneys had no town residence, and it was by no means easy to rent one during term.[1] Roland Whyte, the family steward, in pursuit of what seemed a useless quest tramped all over London "and

[1] The London Season coincided with the law terms.

doe use all my Friends help in it; as yet we can not speed."[1]

Eventually a house was found in Broad Street, not far from the one in Austin Friars occupied by the two devoted sisters, the Countesses of Warwick[2] and Cumberland, the former aunt by marriage to Sir Robert Sidney. Barbara's chief hope of obtaining her husband's leave lay in the influence of his aunts, Lady Warwick and Lady Huntingdon, for they were ladies of the bedchamber to Queen Elizabeth, and two of her most intimate friends.

Lady Warwick made essay at once, "she told her Majestie the desire your Lordship had to come over for two months, about a very earnest occasion in Law, that concerned the good of your children." To which the Queen replied discouragingly "that the time was too daungerous and that she could not believe you yourself desired it."[3] Detailing this set-back to Barbara Sidney, Lady Warwick advised her to approach Lord Burghley, the Earl of Essex, the Lord High Admiral, and Sir Robert Cecil, as being the most influential men at Court and likely to carry weight with the Queen.

Lady Sidney promised she would, and by way of insinuation presented them with some of her famous "Bore pies," sending two to Sir Robert Cecil, "in hope

[1] *Sydney Papers*, A. Collins.
[2] Ann Russell, d. of Francis, 2nd Earl of Bedford. She married Ambrose Dudley, Earl of Warwick, brother to Sir Robert Sidney's mother.
[3] *Sydney Papers*, A. Collins.

he wil be careful of your leave." The "Bore pies" were eaten and appreciated, being "specially much commended for their well seasoning," but the recipients soon found that compliments anent cookery were insufficient acknowledgment, for Lady Sidney sent every day to remind them of their promise to obtain her husband's leave. Sir Robert Sidney himself began to fear she had let zeal outrun discretion, and wrote to Sir Robert Cecil, saying, "I understand your lordship hath put my wife in comfort, that I shall have leave to return this winter. I humbly beseech your lordship to pardon her presuming so far, and lay the blame upon the care that wives will shew to have of their husbands."

As soon as the Queen arrived in town, Lady Sidney, with her three eldest children, Mary,[1] William, and Katherine, went to Whitehall. There they saw the Lord High Admiral, who made much of the little ones, saying that little Mary was nearly big enough to be a Maid of Honour, and "if it had not bene so busy a time, his best cosen and children should have seen the Queen, but he would tell her of their being at Court"; further, he promised to do his best about Sidney's leave.

Early in November, Roland Whyte told the absent father of a domestic calamity:

"Mrs. Mary hath the mesels, but God be thancked, she is nothing sick withall; the feare we have here is of

[1] Mary, m. Sir Robert Wroth in 1604. She became noted as a patroness of literature and wrote a book called *Urania* in imitation of her uncle, Sir Philip Sidney's *Arcadia*.

BARBARA GAMAGE, WIFE OF SIR ROBERT SIDNEY, AND HER CHILDREN
Reproduced by kind permission of Lord de l'Isle and Dudley, Penshurst Place

my Lady herself, who is apt in this state she now is, for to take them. Yet will she not by any persuasion be moved to keape from her, and with much ado be brought to lie from her. The child herself humbly beseaching my Lady to have a care of her own health as she loved her. Mr. William is very well, and forbears not to come to his sister; for, he saies, his turn wilbe next."

William, however, proved the only member of the family who escaped, though the rest of the children had the complaint so lightly that they were all recovered by the end of the month. Then one morning their mother woke up feverish and with a bad cough, and Dr. Brown being called in pronounced it to be "the very measles." It was a depressing day for the household in Broad Street; Roland Whyte and women anxious; the children unhappy; their mother downhearted because now in her hour of affliction the husband she loved so dearly was far away. The children did their best to make up, the steward coming in for instructions noticed that "my lady receives great comfort by her children, who are continually with her; so is Mr. William that hitherto has escaped."

The hours of that winter day dragged slowly, but at four o'clock a mire-bespattered messenger knocked at the door, and handed in a bundle of letters he had brought from Flushing. No medicine could have done so much to restore Lady Sidney as did the sight of her husband's handwriting. She read and reread his letters, telling those around her that now indeed she was comforted in the thought that though nothing could make up for Sir Robert's absence, the next best thing was to know he had such care of her that he had sent over a special messenger to bring him back news of how she did. The messenger himself was brought upstairs to the room where the sick woman lay in the big four-poster, that she might hear from his own lips of her husband, and send him assurances of her love.

The messenger left; doctor and nurses arrived, and at nine o'clock on the 1st of December, 1595, there came into the world "a goodly fat boy, but as full of the measles in the face as can be." Lady Sidney, proud of her wee son, and happy in the companionship of the other children, made rapid recovery, and interested herself in the question of godparents for the new baby. Both she and Sir Robert wished Lady Rich to be one, for, but for the accident of fate which condemned her to a loveless marriage, Penelope would have been their sister-in-law. Sir Philip Sidney lamenting for his lost bride had celebrated her in verse as "Stella," proclaiming her beauty to the world:

"Queen Virtues Court, which some call Stella's face,
Prepared by nature's choicest furniture,
Hath his front built of alabaster pure,
Gold is the covering of that stately place;
The door, by which sometimes comes forth her Grace,
Red porphyr is, which lock of pearl makes sure;
Whose porches rich, which name of cheeks endure,
Marble mixed red and white do interlace."

Roland Whyte, deputed to visit Lady Rich at her

house in St. Bartholomew's Priory, explained that Sir Robert and Lady Sidney wished her to be "gossip" to their boy, but that as mother and baby had the measles, "neither of you for anything in the world, request her unto it."

Lady Rich hesitated a moment, then said that all danger from infection would be over in eight days, so after that time she would be delighted to stand godmother. Next she wanted to know the godfathers, who jointly with herself were to undertake the responsibility of seeing that in due time the new baby learnt to say his catechism. Roland Whyte replied Lord Mountjoy[1] for one, and Lady Rich agreed sedately that as co-gossip he was quite pleasing to her. From St. Bartholomew's, Roland Whyte next went to Lord Mountjoy's house in Holborn, and finding his lordship at home, preferred Lady Sidney's request that he would be godfather. Lord Mountjoy's chief anxiety concerned the godmother; who was she to be? Roland Whyte replied, "My Lady Rich," whilst his observant eyes noticed that Lord Mountjoy "was much pleased at it; and assuring me, whensoever the day was appointed, he would not fail to be there."

Lady Rich as godmother had the privilege of fixing the day, thereby causing a good deal of trouble; first, she put it off because of a visit to the country, from which she did not expect to return before Christmas Eve; secondly, on the score that Lord Compton, the other godfather, wished it. Roland Whyte, who paid

[1] Charles Blount, Earl of Devonshire and 8th Baron Mountjoy.

several visits to her ladyship at St. Bartholomew's, had a different opinion. Lady Rich's and Lord Mountjoy's mutual pleasure at being co-gossips had not escaped him, and he surmised that the lady wished to look her best, telling Sir Robert that it was "a tetter that suddenly broke out in her fair white forehead, which will not be well in five or six days, that keeps your son from being christened."

Lady Sidney regretted the delay, "But my Lady Rich's desires are obeyed as commandment by my Lady." On New Year's Day the ceremony took place in the great chamber at the Sidneys' house in Broad Street. Lady Rich, Lord Mountjoy, and Lord Compton, the godparents, were present and gave little Robert[1] "three very fair standing bowls all of one fashion, that may be worth £20 apiece." Lady Essex came with her daughter, Elizabeth Sidney; the Countess of Cumberland brought her little girl, Ann Clifford, and the company included "many other gentlewomen and gentlemen, all things were so provided, and they had no cause to fear the measles."

It might have been a long time before Lady Sidney could have shown little Robert to his father, had not the Earl of Huntingdon's death occasioned his recall at the Queen's desire, that he might comfort his widowed aunt and look into her affairs. Barbara and the children delighted in having him home, but it was not for long; all too soon he received orders to return to his post. "I see Flushing must be the grave of

[1] Robert Sidney, 2nd Earl of Leicester, d. 1677.

my youth, and I fear my fortune also," he said despondingly.

Next year found Lady Sidney back in London, this time at a house in the Strand, striving hard to obtain another holiday for the reluctant Governor of Flushing. Relatives and friends lent their aid, but the Queen could not be prevailed on to say either yea or nay. Lady Warwick, doing her uttermost, could give no definite encouragement in her letters, though she bid her nephew hope for the best.

"Good Nephew,

"I have received twoe or three verie kinde letters from you, which as I am willinge to requitte, so have I thought good to lett you know what the Queen saith concerning this overthrowe of the Spaniards, which she hath heard of, and of the same good success she is verie gladd of, although she will nott thanck you for your beinge there, yett I doubt not butt that it will be easelie satisfied by my Lord of Essex, and your coming over furthered, whereof I would be as gladd, as I will be of effectinge of any thing you shall desire. And so comend-inge me verie hartilie to you, I do with my well wishing, bid farewell. From the Court the XXI. of January 1596.

Your loving and assured Aunte,

ANNE WARWICK."[1]

Lady Warwick's congratulations proved premature, for on second thoughts, Elizabeth decided to blame

[1] Sydney Papers.

Sidney for allowing the Spanish ships to pass, and the possibility of his obtaining leave seemed more remote than ever.

Roland Whyte wrote constantly to tell Sir Robert how Lady Sidney and her friends laboured on his behalf, and how little they could prevail. Of a more pleasing nature were the steward's accounts of the children:

"Mrs. Mary is grown so tall and goodly of her yeares, as that your Lordship cannot beleve yt, unless you saw yt; and surely will prove an excellent creature. My Lady sees them well taught, and brought up in Learning and Qualities, fitt for theire Birth and condicion.

"Mr. William Sidney, Mrs. Mary and Mrs. Katren; attended the ladies at their coches, and brought them up to my Lady, with an excellent behavior and grace.

"Your son Robert is a young gallant, who for wit and courage gives all men cause to wonder at his yeares, God bless hym, for he will prove a singular man.

"All the children are well, save Mrs. Betty, who is troubled with a good cold, and burns much.

"On St. Stephen's day, in the afternoon, Mrs. Mary danced before the Queen two galliards, with one Mr. Palmer, the admirablest dancer of this time; both were much commended by her Majesty; then she (Mrs. Mary) danced with him a coranto. The Queen kissed Mr. William Sidney in the presence, as she came from the chapel; my lady Warwick presented him.

"The 3 greater children doe very much rejoice in the Remembrance you please to have of them. My Lady

64

Huntingdon told me yester night, that the Queen doth often speak of them, and that she never saw any child come towards her, with a better or bolder grace, than Mrs. Katharine did."

Sometimes the steward, before he closed his letter, would add a message from his mistress: "She commands me to tell you, that you daily give her cause to say, that you are the best Husband in the world, for your love and care towards her, and your children."

At length, after months of alternate hope and despair, Lady Sidney could bear the separation no longer, beseeching Sir Robert to let her and the children join him at Flushing. The children proved the chief obstacle to this plan, for there were now seven of them, and not one would their mother leave behind. Sir Robert, quite willing she should bring the four little ones, wished the three eldest to remain in England, and wrote to his wife on the subject.

"Sweet Hart,
"By Captain *Brown, Davy*, and *Patrick*, I have received 4 letters from you. I am glad to heare thate you, and all my children are well; and for your coming over, I desire it as much as you; and would not let you have bin so long from me, but in respect of your own unfitnes to come over, and the hope I had to have gotten ere this into *England*. But heerein I wel perceive the practis of those, which like not my company at the Court; and I trust, if all things fall out wel, that they

65

shall have done me no hurt in it. Touching your coming over, toward the Middle of *May*, I will send Capt. *Goring*, and Capt. *Brown*, and a couple of Men of Warr from hence; if you do not desire rather to come over in one of the Queen's ships; and therin your own credit is sufficient with my Lord Admiral; and for the bringing over of your children, I am stil of my first Opinion, that I thinck it very unfite to bring the three bigger ones; I know your delight in them, makes you not care, what is best for them; and rather than you will part with them, you will not heare of any place, where to leave them behind you. Otherwise you know wel enough, whoe hath bin desirous to have them, and where they should bee as wel looked unto, as they can be in your own House, and more to their Good, and less to my charges. I meene for the Girls with my Lady of Hunting-ton, and my Lady of Warwick, with whom also you told me you were willing to leave them. They are not so yong now, but that they may wel bee from their mother. Mary is almost ten, and Kate almost eight; and though I cannot find fault hether unto, with their Bringing up, yet I know now every Day more and more, it wil bee fit for them to bee owt of their Father's Hows. For heer they cannot learne, what they may do in other Places; and yet, perhaps, take such Humors, which may be hurtful for them heerafter. But you wil not want Perswaders not to let them, to goe from you, who thinck they shall loose some of their own interest, if they were not abowt the children. But there is not any thing that makes me speake so much, as the experience I have

66

of the Dangerousness of the Aire heer, especially for yong children, whoe have bin accustomed to good Aires; and truth if yow do bring them over, if any thing happen amis to any of them, you shall heerafter not have your wil more in it. For the Boy, I would faine have him with Sir Charls Morison, both in Respect of himself, and for other Reasons also, which when I see you, I wil tel you. For I know there shall bee care had of him there, as much as I would wish. And in the meane time I pray you disuse him from lying with his Mayd. For it is not good for him, and I will have him taken from it. I know that these things are nothing pleasing to you; but you must remember, I have Part in them, as wel as yow, and therefore must have care of them. I know also, that a better, and more careful mother there is not, then you are; and indeed, I doe not feare any thing so much as your to much Fondnes. But having so many as now God hath sent you, you may wel spare the Bigger, and mind them which be yonger; especially that being where I am, yow may the better want their company. But let me heare of this presently, and yow shall receave Answer before yow can come over. Touching *Studley*, though I thinck he little knowes what belongs to a Howskeepers Place, yet since you are to take care of the Hows, and that you are so earnest for him, I wil refer it unto you; but an Upholster were far fitter, though he had more wages, for in worck, which otherwise must be payd for, the wages would bee gotten up again. *Francys* hath bin my servant so long, and my Father's also, as I may not cast him of, now in his old yeares: If hee have offended you, he shall aske your Forgivenes, and you shal remit the offence to me. A chamber also I wil have him have for himself in the Hows: But it is not my meaning he should keepe any Family there; all other things I wil write to you in another letter. And so sweet Hart Farewell. At *Flushing* the 20 of *April* 1597.

Your assured Husband,
R. SYDNEY."[1]

Superscribed:

"To my most dear Wiffe, My Lady *Sydney*."

Remonstrance proved useless. Sir Robert might have an obedient wife in most respects, but when it came to parting with any of her children she was adamant, and leave the three eldest ones behind she would not. They even went with their mother when she drove down to pay a final visit to Penshurst to see that all was in order at the country house, where it was her pride:

> "To have her linen, plate, and all things nigh,
> When she was far; and not a room, but drest
> As if it had expected such a guest."[2]

Back in London Lady Sidney superintended the packing of her household goods, that all might be in readiness when Sir Robert could send ships to bring his family over. On the 2nd of June 1597 Roland Whyte wrote that these had arrived:

"The 2 ships you sent for my Lady are at Gravesend, the Captens have been with her. Upon Monday, God

---

[1] *Sydney Papers.*   [2] *The Forest.*

willing, she begins her journey towards you; she will imbarque her nursery, I meane the 4 little ones, at Gravesend, Herself with the 3 greater, will goe to Margate, where one of the Queen's ships by my Lord Admiralls special care doth attend her."

Lady Sidney soon had reason to wish she had taken her husband's advice and left the elder children behind, for his fears about the unhealthiness of the climate proved only too well founded, and little William became seriously ill. The mother's one anxiety was to get her child back to England and consult the best London doctors. Friends at home, anxious to do all they could, began again the weary business of trying to obtain leave for Sir Robert. Once the Queen granted it, and hopes rose high; next she retracted, and the case seemed hopeless; then she relented and said he might come.

Meanwhile Roland Whyte went up and down the town trying to find a house, but "all the Houses near Charing Cross and Holborn were taken up." Though he "left few Houses unsought for and yet can heare of none fit for you to life in."

In this extremity Sir Robert's sister, Lady Pembroke,[1] came to the rescue, for she and "all your frends here do thincke, that if Mr. William be able to put to sea, that the change of air for recovering of his health, as

---

[1] Mary Sidney, "Sidney's sister, Pembroke's mother," to whom her brother Philip dedicated his *Arcadia*, which she revised and edited for publication. She was a famous Hebrew scholar and a patroness of poets.

they say it is a pity that soe sweet sowls should live in so dangerous an aire." The Earl and Countess of Pembroke lived in the country, rarely using their town residence, Baynard's Castle,[1] on the banks of the Thames, so she gave orders that it should be prepared for Sir Robert and Lady Sidney, that at any rate there should be a house in town to bring little William to. Roland Whyte, very glad indeed to have found something at last, wrote to tell Sir Robert: "I do prepare Baynard's Castle for you, where you shall have all the rooms upon the water side for my lady and the children."

If Lady Sidney and her children looked out of their windows overlooking the Thames on December 28th, 1598, they would have seen a strange sight, for on that day the Lord Chamberlain's company of players, prevented by Lady Russell from acting in the Blackfriars, and unable to renew their lease of "The Theatre," determined to remove the playhouse itself to a site near the Bear Garden at Southwark. Therefore on the 28th of December Richard Burbage and his companions did "ryoutouslye assemble themselves together, and then and there armed themselves with dyvers and many unlawful and offensive weapons, as namely, swordes, daggers, billes, axes, and such like, and soe armed, did

---

[1] Baynard's Castle was built by Humphrey, Duke of Gloucester, in 1428. Richard, Duke of Gloucester, resided there.

   Glo. If you thrive well, bring them to Baynard's Castle;
       Where you shall find me well accompanied
       With reverend fathers and well-learned bishops.
                       (*Richard III*, III, 5.)

then and there repayre to the sayd Theater and . . .
attempted to pull downe the sayd Theater . . . and
having so done did then alsoe in most forcible and
ryotous manner take and carrye away from thence all
the wood and timber thereof unto the Bancksyde in the
parish of St. Marye Overyes, and there erected a newe
play-house with the sayd timber and wood."[1]
During the months that followed, Lady Sidney and
her children looking across the river would see the
building of the Globe Theatre on the Bankside.

[1] *Shakespeare's England*, vol. ii, p. 291.

CHAPTER VI

AMONGST the friends who came to Baynard's Castle to inquire after the now convalescent William was little Robert's beautiful godmother, Penelope Rich. Had things followed as her father wished, Lady Rich would have been the aunt of her small godson, for the Earl of Essex's dying message to Sir Philip Sidney was: "Tell him I send him nothing, but I wish him well, and so well that, if God so move both their hearts, I wish that he might match with my daughter. I call him son. He is wise, virtuous, and godly; and if he go on in the course he hath begun, he will be as famous and worthy a gentleman as ever England bred."

Fate and Penelope's guardian, the Earl of Huntingdon, ruled otherwise. Sidney was poor, and when Lord Rich, "a man of an independent fortune and a known estate, but otherwise of an uncourtly disposition, unsociable, austere, and of no agreeable conversation to her," offered himself as suitor, the Earl of Huntingdon accepted him on behalf of his ward. Penelope herself protested bitterly against an enforced marriage to a man she hated, but remonstrance, passion, and tears were of no avail, and when Sidney returned to Court

72

after a visit to his sister, Lady Pembroke, he found his destined bride had become the wife of "the rich Lord Rich." With bitter irony he played on Penelope's new name:

"Towards Aurora's court a nymph doth dwell
Rich in all beauties which man's eye can see;
Beauties so far from reach of words that we
Abase her praise saying she doth excel:
Rich in those gifts which give the eternal crown;
Who, though most rich in these and every part
Which makes the patents of true worldly bliss,
Hath no misfortune but that RICH she is."

The fact that Penelope was now the wife of another man increased rather than lessened Sidney's love.

"Her, he did love, her he alone did honor
His thoughts, his rimes, his songs were all upon her."[1]

In a series of Sonnets entitled "Stella" he sang of his love; for Penelope "he made hymns of immortal praise"; on her "he spent the riches of his wit."

As Penelope, in her newly married dignity, held an appointment among the ladies of the Queen's privy chamber, Sidney had many opportunities of seeing her, and these chance encounters became the object of his life. Sometimes they were tantalizingly brief: a bevy of horsewomen "by hard promise tied," riding along a dusty road whilst the scorching noonday sun beat down on them. All the ladies, save one, wore black riding-masks and sought further to protect their complexions

[1] Spenser's *Astrophel and Stella.*

by shading their faces with their long plumed fans;
only Lady Rich rode barefaced ; "yet were the hid and
meaner beauties parched," whilst she, "the daintiest
of all, though bare went free":

> "The cause was this;
> The sun, which other's burned, did her but kiss."

Another day Lady Rich went up by water from
Whitehall to London, being rowed in one of the
wherries which the Thames watermen plied for hire
on the Thames. Lucky river! lucky waterman! lucky
boat! thought Sidney.

> "The boat for joy could not to dance forbear
> While wanton winds, with beauties so divine
> Ravished, stayed not till in her golden hair
> They did themselves, Oh sweetest prison, twine."

Once the lover caught a glimpse of "truly richest
Lady Rich, in riches of fortune not deficient, but of
body incomparably riche; of mind most rich,"[1] as she
drove through the streets to attend some Court function.
Running footmen made way for the resplendent coach,
wherein sat the most beautiful woman in London.
As the coach passed Sidney, the page-boy's torch flared
up, and for a moment he saw a vision of golden hair
sparkling with jewels, and a lovely face framed in a
filmy lace ruff ; then the torch flickered down, and
the cavalcade passed by, leaving the watcher cursing
"the page from whom the bad torch fell"; the night

[1] Dedication to Lady Rich in second book of Montaigne's
Essays.

for being so dark; and the coachman "that did drive so fast."

Everything that came near Penelope was to be envied; Sidney, jealous of the attention she paid her pets, asked, "Dear, why make you more of a dog than me?" Lady Rich, cuddling her long-eared pet, replied, because he was loving, patient, faithful, and could do tricks. Sidney said he could supply all those wants quite as well, if not better than a dog:

> "If he do love, I burn, I burn in love;
> If he wait well, I never thence would move.
> If he be fair, yet but a dog can be;
> Little he is, so little worth is he;
> He barkes, my songs thine own voice oft dost prove;
> Bidd'n, perhaps, he fetchèd thee a glove,
> But I, unbid, fetch even my soul to thee
> Yet, while I languish, him that bosom clips,
> That lap doth lap, nay, lets, in spite of spite,
> This sour-breath'd mate taste of those sugar'd lips."

One glorious May-day the lovers met and talked over the hard fate which had riven their young lives asunder. Sidney urged his passionate love, whilst Penelope, though the lovelight shone in her black eyes, strove to calm him. Every word his adored Stella spoke was branded in Philip's memory, and after she had left him he wrote down in verse the result of their all-too-brief interview:

> "In a grove most rich of shade,
> Where birds wanton music made;
> May then young his pied weeds showing,
> New perfumed with flowers fresh growing;

75

Astrophel with Stella sweet
Did for mutual comfort meet,
Both within themselves oppressed,
But each in the other blest.

Him great harms had taught much care,
Her fair neck a foul yoke bare;
But her sight his cares did banish,
In his sight her yoke did vanish.

Wept they had, alas the while,
But now tears themselves did smile
While their eyes, by love directed,
Interchangeably reflected.

.   .   .   .   .   .

Then she spake: her speech was such
As, not ears, but heart did touch;
While such wise she love denied
As yet love she signified.

Astrophel, said she, my love
Cease in these effects to prove.
Now be still; yet still believe me
Thy grief more than death would grieve me.

If that any thought in me
Can taste comfort but of thee,
Let me feed, with hellish anguish,
Joyless, hopeless, endless languish.

If those eyes you praisèd be
Half so dear as you to me,
Let me home return stark-blinded
Of those eyes, and blinder-minded.

76

If to secret of my heart
I do any wish impart
Where thou art not foremost placed,
Be both wish and I defaced.

If more may be said, I say,
All my bliss in thee I lay;
If thou love, my love content thee,
For all love, all faith is meant thee.

.   .   .   .   .   .

Therefore, dear, this no more move,
Lest, though I leave not thy love,
Which too deep in me is framed,
I should blush when thou art named.

Therewithal away she went,
Leaving him to passion rent
With what she had done and spoken,
That therewith my song is broken."

Penelope's pleading prevailed, and Sidney, realizing that she was beyond his reach, married Frances Walsingham,[1] who loved him dearly, and nursed him devotedly after he received his death wound at Zutphen in 1586.

Sidney's death ended the first, but not the last, romance of Penelope's life, for as years passed the gulf between her and her husband widened, and she saw less and less of him. She was fond of her children, but they could not hold her as Barbara Sidney's little ones held their mother. They might be part of her life,

[1] D. of Sir Francis Walsingham, a famous statesman. In 1590, Frances m. Robert, Earl of Essex, thus becoming sister-in-law to Lady Rich.

but they were not the whole of it. Satisfied that the "rich Lord Rich" could supply them with nurses and all material comforts, Penelope threw aside household cares, and flung herself into the whirl of social gaiety. At Court balls, theatrical performances, banquets, and private parties, Lady Rich, easily the most beautiful woman present, was the cynosure of all eyes. Many a man watching the magnificently gowned woman enter the room, her sparkling black eyes looking for friends, recalled Sidney's lines:

"She comes and straight her shining twins do move
Their rays on me!"

Those wonderful eyes! no other woman could boast their equal; a glance from them would set any man's heart athrob:

"When nature made her chief work, Stella's eyes,
In colour black, why wrapt she beams so bright?
Would she in beamy black, like painter wise,
Fame daintiest lustre, mixt of shades and light?
Or did she else that sober hue devise
In object best to knit and strength our sight;
Least, if no veil these brave gleams did disguise,
They, sunlike, should more dazzle than delight?
Or would she her miraculous power show,
That, whereas black seems Beauty's contrary,
She even in black doth make all beauties flow?
Both so, and thus—she, minding Love should be
Placed even there, gave him this mourning weed
To honour all their deaths who for her bleed."

Lady Rich's black eyes caught and held those of Lord Mountjoy, who had been co-gossip with her at little

LADY RICH
From the picture in Lambeth Palace
Reproduced by the kind permission of the Archbishop of Canterbury

Robert Sidney's christening. She found him "courtly, grave, and exceeding comely"; nor was she the only woman of the opinion, for Queen Elizabeth herself had advanced the young man to the position of favourite. At first Her Majesty's chief favourite, Robert, Earl of Essex, had been highly indignant that the Queen's favour should be shown to any one but himself, and challenged the presumptuous young man to a duel. Honour being satisfied, the combatants shook hands, and henceforward were sworn friends: thereby Lord Mountjoy had many opportunities of meeting Lord Essex's beautiful sister. Acquaintance ripened into friendship, and friendship into love. Lord Rich had no control over his wilful wife's actions, and though he dared not openly oppose his powerful brother-in-law, the Earl of Essex, was more than half inclined to suspect him of being privy to Penelope's and Lord Mountjoy's infatuation for each other.

Lady Rich ceased to conform to her marriage vows, though she still visited her husband occasionally, and once, hearing he was dangerously ill, went to nurse him back to health. As soon as the patient recovered, his wife and nurse returned to her lover. Relatives and friends seemed to have acquiesced at the state of affairs, for, though they might chide Penelope for being an "idle housewife," they did little to promote better relations between her and the man whose name she bore. Even Barbara Sidney, devoted wife and mother that she was, asked Lady Rich and Lord Mountjoy to be co-gossips to her little son.

79

Probably the general extenuation was that the marriage was none of Penelope's making: "A lady, of great birth and virtue, being in the power of her friends, was by them married, against her will, unto one against whom she did protest at the very solemnity, and ever after; between whom, from the first day, there ensued continued discord, although the same fears that forced her to marry constrained her to live with him. Instead of a comforter, he did study in all things to torment her; and by fear and fraud did practise to deceive her of her dowry."[1]

Thus matters stood in 1599 when the Earl of Essex, accompanied by a large following, went over to quell the rebellion in Ireland. During his absence Essex lent his country house, Chartley, on the borders of Staffordshire, to his sister Penelope and her cousin, the young Countess of Southampton, recently Maid of Honour to the Queen, who had got herself so grievously into trouble for marrying the Earl of Southampton.[2]

In every way the cousins and devoted friends were unlike; and self-willed, independent Lady Rich must have wondered at the clinging, docile obedience of little Lady Southampton, who desired only to obey her husband in all things. Bitterly she accused herself of

[1] "A Discourse written by the Earl of Devonshire in Defence of his Marriage with the Lady Rich." In 1605 Lord Rich divorced his wife, who then married Mountjoy:

[2] Henry Wriothesley, 3rd Earl of Southampton; m. Elizabeth Vernon 1598. Shakespeare dedicated to him *Venus and Adonis* (1593) and *Lucrece* (1594).

having caused his misfortunes and imprisonment by
the angry Queen, incensed that a young man so distinguished by royal attentions as the Earl of Southampton
had been, should presume to fall in love with any one
but herself. At Essex's earnest solicitation the Earl of
Southampton had been released from prison and allowed
to proceed with the army to Ireland, on the strict
understanding that he should occupy a subordinate
position. This restriction Essex violated immediately
on arriving in Ireland, when he appointed the Earl of
Southampton to be Master of the Horse.

The two women at Chartley waited anxiously for
news, but the posts were irregular, and being so far
from London they did not, probably for their own
peace of mind, hear the rumours which circulated round
the town by word of mouth. Lady Rich hated the
country and longed to be back in London again; Lady
Southampton thought all places where the Earl of
Southampton was not arid deserts, and did not care
where she was. To break this monotonous existence
came a letter from Lord Rich, who still kept up correspondence with his wife, urging her to come to London
as he was threatened with a lawsuit, and thought that
the sister of the all-powerful Earl of Essex would carry
more weight than the "rich Lord Rich" and his money-
bags. Penelope, heartily weary of the country, half
inclined to go, especially as the lawsuit would involve
the interests of her children. Lady Southampton proved
the chief difficulty; Penelope could not very well leave
her behind at Chartley, but the young wife, as subject

to her Lord as Penelope was independent of hers, could hardly be prevailed to trouble him about such an insignificant subje&t as herself. At length, by her cousin's persuading, she wrote in all humility to ask his will:

"My deare Lorde and only joye of my life, bechieh you love me ever, and be pleased to knoe, that my La: Riche wil nides have me send you word howe importunat my Lo: Riche is with her to come to London, fearing he shall lose most of his lande which my Lo: Chamberlain hopes to recover, but he thinkes if she wer heare (in) London she wolde make means to have the suit not presed til his brother's coming home, which else he fears wil goe on to his loues befor that time; therefore goe to him nides she must. She is, she tels me, very loth to leave me heare alone, and most desirus, I thank her, to have me with hir in Essex tel your retorne unto me, and teles me she hath written both to you and hir brother that it may be so. For myselfe I protest unto you that your wil is, ether in this or any thing elce, shale be most plesing to me, and my minde is alike to all plasis in this il time to me of your absence from me, being quiat in no plase. I pray you resolve what you wil have me do, and send me worde of it. If you wil have me goe with hir, she desires that you wil write a letter to my lorde Riche, that I may do so, and she hath sent to hir brother to do the like, for she ses she knows his (h)oumer so wel as he wil not be pleasde unless that corse be taken. She wil be gon before Bartholmy daye therefore before let me I pra you knoe your pleasure what I shall do, which no earthly power shal make me disobaye; and what you dislike in this letter I bechieh you lay not to my charge, for I protest unto you I was most unwilling to give you case of trobel with thinking of any such matter for me in your absence, but that she infinitely desired me to do it; and this lastly protesting unto you againe, that ever you like best I should be, that plas shal be most plesing to me, and all others to be in most hatful to me, I end never ending to praye to God to kepe you ever from all dangers parfitly wel and sone bring you to me, whoe wil endlisly be your faithful and obedient wife.

E. SOUTHAMPTON.

CHARTLY *the* 8 *July*.

All the news I can send you that I thinke wil make you mery is that I read in a letter from London that Sir John Falstaf is by his Mrs. Dame Pintpot made father of a godly millers thum, a boye thats all heade and verie litel body; but this is a secrit."[1]

Lady Rich also wrote to her husband, but she did not sign herself either his loving or obedient wife.

[1] Hist. MSS. Com. iii.

CHAPTER VII

WHEN Lady Rich and Lady Southampton arrived in London, the audiences at the newly opened Globe Theatre on the Bankside were thundering plaudits at a topical allusion in Mr. William Shakespeare's play, *King Henry V*. Wishing to convey an idea of King Henry's return from France, the dramatist bade his hearers imagine the scene that would be enacted in contemporary London when the Earl of Essex returned from Ireland:

> "But now behold,
> In the quick forge and working-house of thought,
> How London doth pour out her citizens!
> The mayor and all his brethren, in best sort,
> Like to the senators of the antique Rome,
> With the plebeians swarming at their heels,
> Go forth and fetch their conquering Cæsar in:
> As by a lower but loving likelihood,
> Were now the general of our gracious empress,
> As in good time he may, from Ireland coming,
> Bringing rebellion broached on his sword,
> How many would the peaceful city quit
> To welcome him!"[1]

Unfortunately, though as yet the public did not

[1] *King Henry V*, Act v, Prologue.

84

know it, the Irish Campaign was going very badly, and there appeared little prospect of Essex returning with "rebellion broached on his sword." The Queen, distressed at the ill-success of her army, and furious with Essex for making the Earl of Southampton Master of the Horse in direct contradiction to her known wishes, wrote such bitter letters to the lord-general that he was convinced they were composed by his rival, Sir Walter Raleigh.

To his anxious wife, waiting for trustworthy news, Essex sent a special messenger, that he might satisfy her by word of mouth concerning things which Her Majesty's lord-general of Ireland dared not commit to paper. "Frank. I send you Cuffe, my man, whom you may believe," he wrote in his letter, adding bitterly, "The Queen's commandment may break my neck, but mine enemies shall never break my heart."

Lady Essex strove to carry a brave face to the world, a task lessened by the fact that it was not the first time she had acted a part. A warm-hearted woman who loved deeply, Frances Walsingham had the hard fate to play second fiddle to two husbands. She married Sir Philip Sidney knowing full well that in his eyes no other woman could usurp the place Stella held in his heart. Yet in the hour of death, Frances claimed him; Lady Rich remained in England, but Sidney's "most dear and loving wife" went over to the Netherlands to nurse her husband on his dying bed.

Four years later Frances remarried, and this time her husband, Robert, Earl of Essex, held pride of place as the Queen's chief favourite, so there was danger as well as jealousy in the bride's position. As every one expeted, Elizabeth was furiously angry, and not even Essex could stem the torrent of her wrath. He was not sent to prison, as Raleigh and Southampton were for a like offence of taking unto themselves wives, but he had to walk warily, "concealing his marriage as much as so open a matter may be; not that he denies it to any, but for her Majesty's better satisfaction is pleased that my lady shall live very retired in her mother's house."[1]

Eventually Elizabeth forgave her favourite, but, as usual, the pardon did not extend to the woman who had presumed to enter the lists as her rival. Like Elizabeth Throckmorton and Elizabeth Vernon, the presumptuous Maids of Honour who had dared to marry Sir Walter Raleigh and the Earl of Southampton, Lady Essex never regained the royal favour. Not being ambitious for political power like Lady Raleigh, Frances would willingly have lived a retired life, happy in the society of her husband, if only she could have kept him to herself. Unfortunately, with the Earl in constant attendance on the Queen, this could not be, and Frances suffered the embittered jealousy of knowing that her husband, always susceptible to feminine charms, was in close proximity to the far too fascinating Maids of Honour. The Earl's flirtations occasioned quarrels between husband and wife, but Frances, though passionate, soon forgave, and once when the Earl left England without bidding her farewell, she wrote:

[1] Lodge's *Illustrations*, vol. ii.

"I thank you for your kind sending which does satisfy me for that unkindness which I took for your going away without taking leave of me. My mother told me it was by her advice, but I did not give so great credit to her speech as I do to your letter. The charge you have laid upon me shall make me strive to overcome those extreme passions which my affeƈtion hath brought me to, and I will have more care of my self for your little ones sake. I am so extreme lame and selie (with) intolerable pain of my head and face that I am almost blind, and therefore must desire you to excuse my briefness and I hope to be better able to write by the next messenger. Farewell, dear life, and make me to be assured of your love have care of yourself. In your absence, I will spend my time in praying for you. My little jewel begins to mend so that I trust within these two or three days he will be well."

The Earl was not a good letter-writer, but in August 1599 Frances could joyfully tell her friends she had "had the good fortune to receive two letters." They were the more welcome because she had been ill, and writing to thank her husband, told him: "The first came when I was so sick that I could not speak with Mr. Darci which brought it, but the joy which I took in receiving news from you did deliver me out of a fever." The precious letters were read and reread, before they were placed in "a casket of reasonable bigness," which always stood by her bedside, and contained all the letters written to her by the Earl during their secret courtship and in later times of his absence.

When her anxiety for news became unbearable, Lady Essex visited such friends as she had among the lords of the Privy Council, or Lady Russell in the Blackfriars, who as Secretary Cecil's aunt, might have secret information. When none could satisfy her anxiety she wrote to the Earl of Southampton in Ireland:

"I will not be in your debt for a letter lest you take occasion to grow slothful and so deprive me of the contentment which your letters bring me. I do infinitely long to hear of my lord's happy proceedings against the proud rebels, which to acquaint me with, you shall do me a great favour. This place yields no matter worth the writing. I will only desire you to esteem my affection, which you shall ever have interest in."

Unfortunately the proceedings against the "proud rebels" were anything but happy, and London was full of sensational rumours on every side. In Westminster Hall, the Royal Exchange, and the middle aisle of St. Paul's Cathedral, where men of all sorts, trades, and occupations congregated, meeting friends, making bargains, showing off new fashions, "What's the news?" was questioned on every side.

> "If it be named newes, 'tis good enough.
> One saies a traveller (a friend of his)
> Is new come home, and he hath told him this:

> Another saies, as he in Paules did walke,
> He heard the newes whereof two knights did talke:
> Another, he hath newes is very rare,
> And heard it sitting in a barber's chaire:
> Another, he is furnish't very strange
> With newes new taken up at the Exchange."[1]

Once started, news circulated by word of mouth, and as it lost nothing in the telling, the town was full of alarming reports. It was said the Army in Ireland had been defeated; that the King of Scotland had invaded the North of England; the Army and Navy were being mobilized; the Spaniards were coming to avenge the defeat of their Armada in '88. London's overstrung nerves gave way when newsmongers confidently asserted that the Spaniards had actually landed in the Isle of Wight, "which bred such a feare and consternation in this towne as I would letel have looked for, with such crie of women, chaining of streets, and shutting of the gates as though the enemie had ben at Blackwal."[2]

Even the redoubtable Lady Russell shared the general alarm, and wrote to her nephew, Sir Robert Cecil, for protection:

"Friend me so much as to procure me a lodging in the Court in this time of misery. Here I remain where none be left but artezans; myself a desolate widow without husband or friend to defend me or to take care of me; my children all in her Majesty's service; myself

---

[1] *Good Newes and Bad Newes*, S. Rowlands.
[2] John Chamberlain's Letters.

so beggared by law and interest for relief of my children as that I was forced to break up my house more than a year since, and to live here with only six, a very few, and those necessary persons, so poor as that on my faith I have not to maintain my private charge till Michaelmas. For God's sake, aid and proteʄt me in this my desolation, and that by your commandment I may have for shot, pikes and halberts on the Queen's price good so many as I shall send for fit to defend my house, promising you that if God deliver me out of this plunge of danger and misery alive, though I be both blind, deaf and stark beggar, yet will I by the experience of this tribulation and discomfort, I will take me to a mischief and marry to avoid the inconvenience of being killed by villains. [*In place of the following phrase which is struck through;* 'marry and be provided of some one that shall defend me, and take care for me living and to bury me, and not thus to live, no man caring for my soul and life, that hitherto all my days have lived in continual care for others.'] *A Domino factum est. Sit nomen Domini benediʄtum.* I beseech you, Sir, advise me what to do, and help to place me in a Court lodging that have no other place to fly unto for safety."

On Michaelmas Day London hummed with news when it became known that the Earl of Essex, leaving his army in Ireland, had arrived in England, and ridden post-haste to the Queen at Nonsuch. News, news, what's the news? What had happened at Nonsuch? that was what all men wanted to know. One rumour said the Queen and Essex were reconciled, and the citizens rejoiced thereat, for they loved their Queen, and had made the Earl their idol. Next followed a report that the Queen was very angry with the Earl and had ordered him to be removed to York House in custody of Lord Keeper Egerton. News, news, what's the news? Who could tell what was true and what false?

During those anxious days when Essex's fate hung in the balance, his wife gave birth to a baby girl. At first Lady Walsingham tried to keep the truth from her daughter, but Frances, somehow or other, heard of her husband's return and would not be pacified. If in England why did he not come and see her? What was it they were keeping back? Lady Walsingham made humble suit to the Queen that her son-in-law might be allowed to visit his wife, or at least to write to her. Both requests were refused, and Lady Walsingham could no longer hide the fact that the Queen was very angry at the Earl's leaving Ireland without permission, and had placed him under close restraint.

So soon as she could rise from her bed, Lady Essex, dressed all in black of the cheapest material, to denote her humility and distress, went about from one in-fluential friend to another begging them to intercede with the Queen. They could give but little comfort, though they, and all men, grieved to see her going about the town, shorn of all her former state as a Countess, and wife of the famous Earl of Essex. Roland Whyte saw her several times, and with genuine sorrow he wrote to Sir Robert Sidney:

" My Lady of Essex is a most sorrowful creature for her husband's captivity; she wears all black of the meanest price, and receives no comfort in anything. She is most desirous to see her lord, but he is resolved, as they say, to see no creature but such as came from the queen. Some or other told her of a warrant to send him to the Tower, which infinitely grieves her."[1]

On Sunday, November 25th, Lady Essex went to Court, "all in black, her dress not being value £5," and endeavoured to see the Countess of Huntingdon. It would have been a bitter visit for a proud woman; but Frances was not proud, only a miserable, anxious wife. Courtiers and Court ladies looked askance; even the Countess of Huntingdon, when told the Countess of Essex stood without at her chamber door seeking admission, dared not see her. Lady Essex took the rebuff meekly, but sent back a message praying that her lady-ship would use her influence with the Queen to obtain permission for the Countess of Essex to visit her Lord. The answer returned was "that she must attend Her Majesty's pleasure by the Lords of the Council, and come no more to Court. It was ill taken that she presumed to come, having been denied it long since."

Forbidden the Court, and rendered nearly distracted by the prevalent rumours that her husband was sick almost unto death, "my lady Essex rises almost every day by daylight to go to my Lord Treasurer and Sir John Fortescue, for to Court she may not come."

[1] *Sydney Papers.*

In the end importu ity prevailed, and it was through the medium of Sir R bert Cecil, reputed the Earl of Essex's chief enemy, that the heart-broken wife at length received permission to see her husb.. d. On the 12th December 1599 she wrote to expres her gratitude:

"Simple thankes is a slender recompens (good Mr. Secretary) for so honorable a kindnes as you have done me, in procuringe me her Ma^te gracious consent for my infynitly wished access to my weake lord: yet, when they come from a minde truly desirous to deserve it, and from a person that only wantes ability to requite it, I doubt not but the same vertue that led you to so charitable a worke, will likewise move you to accept in good part so beggarly a tribut. Beeleeve, S^r, I pray you, that as pitty only and no merritt of mine was the true motive of your honorable mediacon on my behalf: so no time or fortune shall ever extingwish in my lord and mee a thankfull memory and due acknowledgment of so undeserved a benefitt, from him whom this frendly favour assures mee will never bee proved my lord's maliceious enemy; the respect of your manifold business makes me forbeare to trouble you longer with my scribled lines, but in thankfullest manner to rest your exceedingly beeholdinge frend,

FRA: ESSEX."[1]

Lady Essex made the most of her opportunity; by seven o'clock each morning she arrived at York House,

[1] Hatfield MSS. ix.

and remained there till six in the evening, when she returned to her mother at Walsingham House in Seething Lane. Under his wife's care the Earl's health improved: "He often walks upon his open leads and in his garden with his wife; and now he, now she reading one to the other."

No one had expected the Earl's disgrace to be of long duration, but to every one's astonishment Elizabeth showed no signs of relenting towards her former favourite. Indeed, she showed increased rigour, for Lady Essex's visits were suddenly stopped "till Her Majesty's further pleasure were known, which was to her an exceeding grief; she wept pitifully." When the visits were renewed the time was curtailed, "for now she comes but at nine in the morning, and stays till four in the afternoon."

One day in May, after leaving her husband, Lady Essex went to pay a visit to Lady Sidney, who was still with her children at Baynard's Castle, though Sir Robert had once more returned to Flushing. Barbara Sidney, at least, was no time-server to turn from her friend because of the Earl's disgrace, and she gave her all the sympathy that a happily wedded wife extends to another trembling with anxiety for the fate of her husband. As they sat in the big room with its narrow, old-fashioned windows, looking out over the river Thames, which washed the walls of Baynard's Castle, they could see the Globe Playhouse where so recently had been foretold the Essex's triumphant return from Ireland. How differently it had turned out from Mr.

Shakespeare's happy invention. Few of those who had vociferously acclaimed the prospect of going out to meet the General "bringing rebellion broached on his sword" dared even to express sympathy with the disgraced Lord Deputy of Ireland.

Kindly Lady Sidney, in her rich dress and lace ruff, could hardly bear to look at her poverty-stricken friend, for "to see her clad as she was, was a pitiful spectacle." To such a sympathetic friend, Lady Essex could open her heart, for she had a terrible private anxiety. On first hearing of the Earl's imprisonment, she had thought of the inlaid cabinet wherein she treasured all the letters her husband had ever written to her. They contained private matters which might be injurious to him if they fell into the hands of his enemies, but Frances could not make up her mind to destroy them. Fearing, however, that her house might be searched, she sent for Jane Rehora, a favourite waiting-woman who had recently married one of the Earl's serving-men named Daniel. To her Lady Essex entrusted the locked cabinet, begging her to take it home and hide it till such a time as her old mistress should send for it again.

Early in January, Lady Essex asked her ex-waiting woman if the casket was safe, to which Mrs. Daniel replied "that it was very safe, and had bene sene of no creature lyving." Though innocently, Mrs. Daniel lied, for she had an inquisitive husband, who finding a locked cabinet under his bed, never rested till he had opened it and examined the contents. Private letters of the disgraced Earl of Essex to his Countess! There was

95

money to be made out of this discovery, and Daniel took certain of the letters to a scrivener requesting him to copy them "as neere and like as he possibly could to the said Earle of Essex proper handwriting."

Lady Essex, at length deeming it safe to have the letters back, sent one of her gentlemen to the Daniels' for the cabinet, which he brought back and gave into his mistress's hands. Delighted to have her treasures once more, Frances unlocked the cabinet, when to her horror and consternation she discovered that several of the letters, and those the most dangerous, were missing. In all haste she went round to the Daniels' house, when Mrs. Daniel positively denied that the casket had ever been tampered with. Daniel, being present, confirmed this, but assumed a hectoring manner to the two frightened women, saying that if the contents of the cabinet were so important both his wife and her mistress had done him an injury by bringing them into the house, "and thereupon very peremptorily began to tax the Countess of some want of noble respect, and his wife of great imprudence and undutifulness, and used other very crafty and subtill and discurteous speeches to the Countess."[1]

Lady Essex replied that the cabinet contained "only letters of affection" from her husband to her, but she feared he "might conceave some mislike against her by careless suffering his letters directed to her to be divulged and spread abroad."

The crafty Daniel pretended to be mollified at this,

[1] *The Egerton Papers.*

96

saying that if that was the case he would endeavour to find the letters, which he thought might have been stolen by a recently dismissed maid.

Later, receiving intimation that Daniel had found the missing letters, the Countess sent word, "Let him bring them to me, and my Lord and I will be better and more kind to him than ever we were." Daniel, who wanted something more material than promises of goodwill from a disgraced Lord and his Lady, did not bring the letters, and Lady Essex in alarm besought Mrs. Jane to try and influence her husband. This she promised to do, saying later on, "If the depth of this matter were well known, I received the like success that Volumnia had in persuading her son Coriolanus to raise the siege from Rome."[1] To her husband, away at Richmond, Jane Daniel wrote, and in due time received reply:

" Jane, I am glad that the Countess of Essex made you acquainted where her letters are, which I was loth to have done. But now I think good to let you know, that my decayed estate is more than I was willing you should be a partaker of; and although I meant to have delivered the Countess' letters to her Majesty, yet if I can recover myself by them that have wrought my decay, I will for your sake, forbear my purpose; hoping the Countess will deal well with me, and recompense all my losses sustained by her and her Lord, then I will

[1] MS. "Daniel's Disasters" discovered in the Chapter House, Westminster. Printed in Jardine's *State Trials*.

willingly satisfy her request in that behalf; otherwise I will deliver her letters to the Queen, as I was before determined, and so do bid you heartily farewell."

Daniel demanded £3000 for the letters, an amount quite beyond the Countess's means, but in her desperation she sold all her jewels greatly under value for £1720. This sum Daniel ungraciously accepted, swearing on his Bible oath that the packet handed over contained all the missing letters, and that no copies had been made.

With trembling fingers Lady Essex opened the packet, giving a cry of dismay when she saw, not the original letters, but forged duplicates, the clever imitation whereof never for a moment deceived the Countess's loving eyes. In her deep distress she consulted certain trustworthy friends, by whose means Daniel was eventually called before the Star Chamber that he "might receive some extraordinary and exemplary punishment."

The Court after considering "the heynousness of the said offences, well waighing the quality and falsetie thereof," declared that Daniel deserved "most severe and condigne punishment" for "the great and intollerable wrong" he had done the Countess of Essex, who as "their Lordships themselves could witness and testifie," had done "as much as was possible for her by all meanes and industrie for the good of her husband in the time of his duress and imprisonment, being ever reputed a most vertuous and ho: Lady."

Daniel was fined £3000, and committed to the Fleet

Prison, "there to remaine all the daies of his life." And that the public might, by the means of rotten eggs and stinking fish, have opportunity to express their abhorrence of such a man, it was further ordained that "the said Daniel shall be set upon the pillory, with his ears thereunto nayled, with a paper on his head inscribed: "For Forgery, Corrupte Cosenage, and other leude practises."[1]

[1] *The Egerton Papers*. Daniel was released at the accession of James I.

CHAPTER VIII

LADY RICH and the Countess of Southampton were at Essex House in the Strand when the Earl of Essex arrived so unexpectedly from Ireland, but hearing that the resort of company to them gave offence to the Queen they immediately left for the country, hoping that things would blow over. As this surmise proved quite incorrect, they returned to town, this time very unobtrusively, for Lady Rich was consumed with anxiety for her disgraced brother, and Lady Southampton none too happy about her lord's safety, for though returned from Ireland he dared not appear at Court, but passed "the tyme in London merely in going to plaies every day."

The two sisters, Lady Rich and Lady Northumberland,[1] dressed in deep mourning, made humble application for permission to see their brother. Roland Whyte, gathering all the news he could to send to Sir Robert Sidney, saw them the day before the Queen left Whitehall for Richmond.

" The two ladies, Northumberland and Rich, all in black, were at Court before the remove; what success

[1] Dorothy Perrot, m. 2nd, Henry, 9th Earl of Northumberland.

they had with her Majesty I do not know; they were humble suitors to have the Earl removed to a better air and to a more convenient place, for where he is somewhat straitly lodged, in respect my Lord Keeper's household is great."

Lady Rich, too impatient for lowly solicitations and consequent rebuffs, sought another way to soften the Queen's heart than by kneeling before her in abject humility:

"The Lady Rich earnestly follows her desire to have leave to go and see him; she writes her Majesty many letters, sends many jewels, many presents. Her letters are read, her presents received, but no leave granted."

These failing, Lady Rich next tried what she could do with Mr. Secretary Cecil:

"Mr. Secretary,
        "The favour you have done my sister of Essex doth both encourage me to be thus importunate, and gives me hope to obtain my suit, if it please you to make me so much beholden unto you as to speak earnestly for me to her Majesty for my leave to visit my brother; and if I have no greater liberty to see him but once, yet I shall be well satisfied and esteem the obligation very great of your kindness in assisting me in this my earnest request. Her Majesty told me that if she granted me leave, my sister would look for as much, which need be

no argument against me, since her Majesty being content to permit that favour but to some few, I may, if (it) please her, obtain it before others because I have humbly and earnestly made the first suit, for which I have laid my hopes upon yourself, and will ever remain, your most affectionate friend,

PENELOPE RICH."[1]

Cecil promised to do what he could, but Lady Rich, considering him her brother's chief enemy, and finding he did not grant her immediate wish, sat down and composed yet another letter to the Queen, in which she plainly hinted that Essex's disgrace had root in Secretary Cecil's ambition. Though written in the strain of extravagant admiration, common to most addresses to her "sacred Majesty," the letter contained considerably more plain speaking than usually reached Elizabeth's eyes and ears.

Lady Rich made several copies of the letter, and being proud of it as a piece of composition, which she imagined would advance her brother's cause, she not only showed it to her intimates, but allowed it to be seen of more people than was prudent, so that it got into print, "which is an exceeding wrong done to the Earl."

So indeed it proved, for when the actual letter was delivered to the Queen, she read it through with rising indignation:

"Early did I hope this morning to have had myne
[1] Hatfield MS. x. p. 21.

102

eyes blessed with your Majestie's butyes, but seeing the sonne desappere into a cloud, and meeting with spiritts that did presage by the wheeles of theyr charriotts som thunder in the ayr, I must complayn and express my feares to the High Majestie and devine oracle from whence I receaved a doubtful answer, unto whose power I must sacrifice agayne and agayne the teares and prayers of the afflicted that must dispayr in tyme if it be too soon to importun Heaven when we feel the miseryes of Hell, or that words directed to your sacred wisdome should be out of season delivered for my unfortunat brother, whom all men have liberty to defame as if his offences were capitall and he so base dejected a creature that his love, his lyfe, his services to your butyes and the state had deserved no absolucion after so hard punishment, or so much as to answer in your fayr presence who would vouchsafe more justice and favor then he can expect of partiall judges, or those combined enemyes that labour upon false grounds to buyld his ruine, urging his faults as criminall to your devine honor, thinking it a heaven to blasphem Heaven when theyr owne particuler malice and counsayle have practized only to glutt themselves in theyr privat revenge, not regarding your servis and losse so much as theyr ambitious ends, to rise by his overthrowe. And I have reason to apprehend that if your fayr hands do not check the course of theyr unbridled hate, that the last course wilbe his last breath, since the evill instruments that by theyr office and cunning provide for the feast have sufficient poison in theyr harts to infect. The servis, they will seem, shalbe easy to digest till it be tasted, then will it prove a preparative of greater mischefe concealed amongst such crafty workmen as will not only pull downe all the obstacles of theyr greatnes, but when they are in theyr full strengths (like gyants) make warr agaynst Heaven. But your Majesties conclusion in giving hope of audience is all the hope and comfort I have, which if you hasten not before he take a full surfett of disgraces, they will say the spotts they have cast upon him are too foule to be washed away, and so his disgraced reputacion must disable him for ever serving agayne his sacred goddess, whose excellent butyes and perfecions will never sufferr those fayr eyes to turn so farr from compassion; but at least, if he may not return to the happyness of his former servis to live at the feet of his admired mistris, yet he may sett downe to a privat lyfe without imputacion of infamye, that then posteritye may not repent theyr fathers were borne to so hard destinye, two of them perishing by being employed in one cuntry when they would have done you servis to the shedding of theyr last bloud if they had not bin wounded to death behind with faccion that careth not upon whose neck they buyld the walles of theyr owne fortunes, which I fear, will grow mor dangerousli high then yet is discovered, if God not hinder the worke as the Tower of Babbell, and confound theyr tongues that understand on another too well. And lastly, since out of your princely nature and unstayned vertue ther must needs appear that good virtues are not far from such butyes, I humbly beseech you to make it your

owne worke and not to suffer those to take advantage
that lye in ambush, thinking, so soon as they discover
a relenting and compassion in your worthy mind, to
take the honor upon them as meanes of our salvacion,
not out of charity but pride, that all must be attributed
to them, and your sacred clemencye abused as by forcing
us to go through purgatory into Heaven. But let your
Majestie's devine power be no more eclipsed then your
butye, which hath shyned through all the world. And
imitate the Highest in not destroying those that trust
allways in your mercyes.

With humble request I presume to kiss your fayrest
hands, vowing all obedience and endless love."[1]

In a right royal temper Queen Elizabeth threw the
offending letter into the fire; sent word to Lady Rich
to consider herself under restraint, and ordered Lord
Treasurer Buckhurst[2] to go and examine her. The Lord
Treasurer, who much disliked the task imposed on
him, delayed so long that he got into trouble himself
for showing lack of zeal in reproving the offending lady,
and could put off the interview no longer. He found
Lady Rich "sickly discontented," but charming as ever,
and so persuasive, that the Lord Treasurer's report
showed such bias in her favour that the Queen was
greatly incensed. She desired her secretary to write
Lord Buckhurst, and tell him plainly "her mislike that
your Lordship did so long defer the matter, and that

[1] Hist. MSS. Com. Various Collections, vii.
[2] Thomas Sackville, 1st Earl of Dorset, 1536–1608.

you were still so apt to excuse my Lady's course in her former answers by imputing that to fear of giving further offence, which rather showed a proud disposition, and not much better than a plain contempt of her Majesty and yourself that was used in the cause."

The defaulting Lord Treasurer put aside State affairs in order to write out an account of his examination of Lady Rich, though even after his own reproof he could not forbear making out the best case possible for the lady. The Queen read the document to herself, but the remarks she made aloud, and which she intended Cecil to report to Lord Buckhurst and thence to Lady Rich, were sufficiently caustic.

The Lord Treasurer reported that Lady Rich had expressed sorrow "for her Majesty's displeasure, her fear to offend further, her humble and obedient spirit to satisfy all doubts and her great desire to recover her Majesty's favour."

And with very good reason too, considered the Queen, telling Cecil to write down: "It is true her Majesty was displeased, as she had cause, to see that she, being a lady to whom it did not appertain so to meddle in such matters; would be so bold to write in such a style to her, especially when the best interpretations, which she doth make, cannot free her from stomach and presumption when she writ, and when her former careless and dry answers shewed how little she valued her Majesty's commandments; but her Majesty saith that as she may well perceive by her manner of proceeding with her, that she hath been far from desire to improve her faults."

Penelope's promises of amendment for the future, if she might have her liberty in the present, sounded so humble when repeated by Lord Buckhurst, that the Queen, slightly mollified, sent word, that having noted Lady Rich's "resolution to carry herself as becomes her to all persons hereafter," she would allow her ladyship "to dispose of herself as may best agree with her own health or other respect." Not that this implied any graciousness towards the culprit; far from it, Elizabeth requiring Cecil to make it quite plain to Lord Buckhurst that "if she took pleasure to find her faulty, howsoever she may free her from direct desire or purpose to have it printed, she is well able to prove when she hath given copies, by which means it hath been printed, and if it was no worse than that she was only so negligent that others might come by it, her error was not so excusable but that shrewd circumstances might be inferred upon such a voluntary negligence."[1]

Lady Rich's "piquant letter" did her brother harm, for since it had been circulated amongst the citizens who "were perfect Idolizers of his virtue,"[2] the Queen resolved to have the Earl brought up before the Lords of the Council at York House on June 5th. Sir Edward Coke, the Attorney-General, whose abusive tongue made him the most feared man in the kingdom, conducted the prosecution. In the course of a bitter speech

[1] Hatfield MSS. x.
[2] *Life and Reign of Queen Elizabeth*, Camden.

107

of accusation against the Earl, he said he considered Lady Rich's letter to the Queen "insolent, saucy and malpert and aggravation of the offence."

The Earl had to wait for another six weeks whilst the Queen considered the report, and wife, sister, and mother lived in an agony of apprehension as to the ultimate verdict. Eventually the lords of the Privy Council announced the result: Essex might consider himself free from restraint, but not from indignation, and to Court he must not come. It was generally thought this prohibition would soon be removed, and the former favourite reinstated in the Queen's good graces. But, to the surprise of Lady Warwick and other Court ladies who endeavoured to further the Earl's cause, the Queen remained obdurate, showing no signs whatever of relenting to the man who for so long had held the first place in her affection.

If the Earl had patience all might come right in time, but, unfortunately, patience none of the Devereuxs possessed. The Queen, though she still clung to the illusion of her perpetual youth, was quite obviously an old woman despite the paint, powder, and wigs with which she fondly supposed she had cheated time and deceived the eyes of her subjects. She had kept up the idea of her eventual marriage till it had become a farce, in which Essex and Mountjoy, who had long given their hearts to younger women, continued to play the parts of the Queen's despairing lovers. But it was only acting, for the players were weary of their parts, and their tributes sounded hollow in the ears of the Queen, whose angry tirades hid an aching heart. Essex, still a young man, might reasonably hope for a brilliant career under Elizabeth's successor. Who that might be exercised all men's minds in secret, for Elizabeth refused either to nominate an heir or allow the subject to be mentioned in her presence. As a natural result, it was mentioned very much indeed in private, and the Earl of Essex had for several years carried on a secret correspondence with King James VI of Scotland through the medium of his sister Penelope.

Lady Rich had embarked on the perilous adventure with zest, and, as it was not safe to mention actual people, Penelope called herself *Rialta*, King James *Victor*, Queen Elizabeth *Venus*, her brother the Earl of Essex the *Weary Knight*, because she said he was "exceeding weary, accounting it a thrall that he now lives in, and wishes the change." In her anxiety to be mysterious, Penelope's letters though very amusing were sometimes difficult to follow, so that King James had to have "the dark parts thereof expounded to him." When he did understand, "he commended much the fineness of her wit, and invention, and well-writing." *Rialta* wrote nearly every week, always assuring James of her brother's adherence to his claim: "This day Mr. Richard showed the King two of her letters and expounded them . . . how much the Earl loves the King and honours him, and would fain the King were so persuaded thoroughly."[1]

If Elizabeth would only have nominated King James

[1] Murdin's *State Papers*.

as her successor he would have been satisfied, but she would do nothing of the sort, and Essex and his sister affrighted him grievously by saying that Cecil, the Lord Admiral, Sir Walter Raleigh, and Lord Cobham were all opposed to his claim. Therefore, when Essex, released from confinement but chafing under disgrace, formed a plan to force his way into the Queen's presence, obtain his own pardon, and compel her to proclaim King James next heir to the throne, he sent messages forthwith to Scotland to invite James's co-operation.

CHAPTER IX

EVERY day Lady Rich's coach drove up to Essex House in the Strand, for, if Penelope had lost social influence through her brother's disgrace, she at any rate remained paramount with him. With his wife's anxiety for peace and safety, Essex might have listened to the wiser counsels of Lady Warwick and other Court friends, who urged that repentance and time would eventually soften the Queen. Proud Penelope scorned such an attitude, and her impetuous tongue lashed out at her brother that he should bethink him of such craven courses. Essex listened and gave way, telling others that his sister "did continually urge me on with telling me how all my friends and followers thought me a coward, and that I had lost all my valour."

The doors of Essex House were thrown open "for all swordsmen, malcontents, and broken gentlemen, and admitted buffoons and parasites of all sorts";[1] whilst in the afternoon certain of the Puritan divines preached sermons, "which the tradesmen mightily frequented."

This concourse at Essex House aroused the suspicion of the lords of the Privy Council, so they sent a message

[1] Camden's *Annales*.

III

ordering the Earl to appear before them. Essex to gain time feigned illness, but he and his fellow-conspirators knew now they must aĉt at once. Meeting in conclave to discuss the situation, they decided that if a rebellion there was to be it must be now or never; yea or nay? The yeas had it.

Aĉtive brains evolved plans: Sunday, February 8th, should be the day appointed, and, to influence the public mind towards rebellion, what could be better than a performance of William Shakespeare's play "of the deposing and killyng of Kyng Rychard the Second," at the Globe Theatre? Lord Mounteagle[1] and other conspirators went to interview the players, "promising to give them 40s. more than their ordynary to play yt." Even the extra forty shillings did not tempt the company, who had already rehearsed another play for Saturday, which they thought would prove more popular than *King Richard II*, a play "so old and so long out of use that they shold have small or no company at yt." Lord Mounteagle persuaded, the aĉtors argued, but eventually gave in, and "were content to play yt the Saterday, and hadd their 40s. more than their ordinary for yt, and so played yt accordingly."[2]

That night when the playgoers were safely in their beds, messengers went up and down the town calling on Essex's friends to join him at his house in the Strand.

[1] William Parker, 4th Lord Mounteagle. Received the letter warning him of the Gunpowder Plot, which led to its deteĉtion.

[2] Examination of Augustine Phillips. Domestic State Papers. Eliz. 278 (85).

On Sunday morning the Earl and his sister took stock of those assembled and noted absentees. Of the latter was the Earl of Bedford, and Lady Rich volunteered to go and fetch him. When her ladyship's coach had passed through the crowd in the courtyard, the gates were locked and bolted.

Nor were they opened when the lords of the Privy Council arrived and demanded admittance. After parley through the wicket, Sir Thomas Egerton, the Lord Keeper, Lord Chief Justice Popham, the Earl of Worcester, and Sir William Knollys, were allowed to come in on the condition that their servants remained outside. The lords, not lacking in courage, agreed, and when the bolts had been withdrawn stepped forward pompously into the crowd of armed men "assembled together in a very tumultuous sort." The conspirators' own followers had been reinforced by "Pauls men,"[1] as the riff-raff swashbucklers, who congregated round Duke Humphrey's tomb in St. Paul's, were called. These desperadoes, the originals of Bardolph, Pistol, and Nym who strutted vaingloriously on the stage of the Globe Playhouse, could be hired for any wild scheme; and they were not at all responsive to authority. Instead of removing their hats and making low obeisance to my lords of the Council, they made "no reckoning of the Lord Keeper, and such as were sent with him," but jostled them roughly, shouting out, "Kill them, kill them! we shall have the fewer to deal with."

[1] Falstaff referring to Bardolph says, "I bought him in Pauls." *Second Part, King Henry IV*, III, 2.

Whatever secret tremors they suffered, the lords of the Council retained their dignity, and when they came up to Essex, Southampton, and other conspirators, the Lord Keeper, acting as spokesman, asked the meaning of this concourse. Essex, murmuring something about his enemies having designs against his life, escorted the four lords into the house. Thinking he intended private conference with them they followed him unsuspiciously into a back room, but once there the Earl's attitude altered, and he informed them briefly that they would be kept as hostages till his return from the city. Therewith he locked the door and departed, leaving orders that "if any violence was offered to the house, or that the Earl of Essex miscarried in London, that the Lord Keeper and the Lord Chief Justice should be presently killed."

Meanwhile Lady Rich, who found the Earl of Bedford at Sunday morning prayers, had brought him back to Essex House in her coach. He had not dared to refuse her ladyship's request for his company, but when he found the house in a state of siege, he became very uneasy and earnestly "desired to convey myself away."[1] He desired it still more when he heard that several of the lords of the Council were imprisoned in the house. No peaceable man with any regard for the safety of his own head would be mixed up in such a business if he could help it. Unfortunately, no one who came into Essex House that Sunday morning could help it, for, once in, there was no getting out again.

At length the gates were opened, and Essex with his

[1] Earl of Bedford to the Privy Council.

followers sallied forth shouting, "For the Queen, for the Queen"; "my Lord of Essex should have been murdered in his bed by Sir Walter Raleigh"; and that the Crown of England was sold to Spain. The citizens just returning from church wondered what it was all about, but showed no inclination at all to join actively in the rebellion. It was a peaceable Sabbath day, and rebellion and treason had an ugly sound.

Lady Rich, excited and confident, and Lady Essex, fearful and desponding, waited anxiously for news. When it came it proved by no means reassuring; the citizens had not joined the rebellion; tradesmen refused to supply arms; the Crown forces were in possession; the city placarded with warrants proclaiming:

"Whereas the Earl of Essex and his confederates have taken arms against the Queen's Majesty, and have this day been proclaimed traitors, and thereby are to be prosecuted as traitors and rebels. These are in her Majesty's name straitly to charge and command you, upon your allegiance, forthwith to arm yourselves as many as can with horse and armour, and the rest as foot with pike and shot, presently to repair hither and with us to march to the Court for the defence of her Majesty's person, or otherwise as you shall be commanded; and the shot to be furnished with bullet, powder and match convenient."

The only people who did not know how matters were progressing were the imprisoned Privy Councillors, for, as Lord Chief Justice Popham complained, "none was suffered to go out from us to report what plight we were in." Neither were their guardians any too considerate at first, for Mr. Francis Tresham,[1] a young man and impertinent, did actually tell the Lord Keeper to his face that "he had stayed two years for a motion in the Chancery, and hoped his Lordship was now at good leisure to hear him."

As reports from the city grew worse, their lordships' gaolers became more civil, for in very truth they liked not their office now that seemingly the Earl's rebellion had miscarried. Presently one of them went upstairs to the room where Lady Essex with her sister-in-law and their gentlewomen were assembled, and besought her to come down and speak to the imprisoned Privy Councillors. Distracted with anxiety, Lady Essex at first refused, saying miserably, "With what comfort can I go amongst them?" Eventually she allowed herself to be persuaded, and went to the prisoners, who when they saw her rose and asked, "What strange course is this the Earl of Essex taketh?" Poor Lady Essex could not satisfy them on this point, only she assured them her lord intended no ill to them or to the Queen. After Lady Essex had left, she caused dinner to be served to the captives, but the hungry Privy Councillors refused to touch it, saying, "We would eat none of my Lord's meat."

Their lordships were now a source of grave embarrassment to the garrison at Essex House, for beyond all doubt the rebellion had failed, and any moment

[1] One of the Gunpowder Plot conspirators.

might bring word of Essex's capture. In this predicament Sir Ferdinando Gorges released the Privy Councillors, and then followed hard on their heels to Court to get what mercy he might for himself.

Soon after their release Essex returned, having hired a boat at Queen Hithe and rowed up to the water-gate at the bottom of his garden. His anxious wife and sister greeted him, but their news of the escaped Privy Councillors destroyed the Earl's last hope, for he had relied on holding them as hostages. There was scant time for words, however, and whilst the Earl destroyed his private papers the house was barricaded for a siege.

The precautions were taken none too soon, for Lord Burghley attacked the house from the street side, and a captain standing at a gallery window received a shot fired from St. Clement's Church, commandeered by the besiegers because it stood opposite the courtyard entrance. Watchers on the riverside reported equally bad news, for through the dusk they could see the Lord Admiral and his men landing at the water-gate and forming groups under the trees. Presently trumpet and drum sounded a parley, and Sir Robert Sidney, just returned from Flushing, and appointed this unwelcome task, came forward to demand the rebels' surrender.

The Earls of Essex and Southampton came out on to the leads, endeavouring to obtain permission for Essex to go in person to the Queen and lay his case before her.

"My Lord, you must not capitulate with your Prince," replied Sidney, knowing full well that the Lord Admiral would never consent to this proposition.

" Good Cozin, I do not capitulate with my Prince, I do but expostulate a little with you," said Southampton.

Against his will, and well knowing the futility of it, Sir Robert Sidney eventually agreed to return to the Lord Admiral with the Earl's request. Watchers in the house saw him disappear into the darkness; a little later he emerged from the shadows and sounded a second parley. Heavy-hearted at the fate of his friends, Sir Robert could only tell them that the Lord Admiral refused their request, and that he had sent for powder and ordinance to blow up the house. Raising his voice that it might carry to the listeners on the roof, he conveyed the Lord Admiral's message, "but because he understands that your ladies are in the house with you, to the end that the innocent may not perish with the guilty, for so he esteemeth your ladies with your gentlewomen, he willeth you to send them forth, and they shall be safely and honourably conveyed to some other place, that they shall both like of."

The Earls would have been only too glad of this safe conduct for Lady Essex and Lady Rich, with their waiting-women, "who fill'd the place with their shrieks and cries," but feared that to let the ladies out would be to let their enemies in. If the Lord Admiral would grant "but one hour space to open the passage for our ladies going out, and one other hour space to fortify it again, with promise, upon his honour not to make any attempt upon us in the mean time, then we will willingly suffer our ladies to depart."

Sidney promised this should be granted, but urged

the Earls to surrender themselves, for powder and ordinance had arrived from the Tower, and when the promised time had expired the Lord Admiral would batter down the house. Essex and Southampton retired within for consultation with their friends; some were for surrender; others for cutting their way out. The former carried the day, and presently the doors of Essex House were opened to admit the Lord Admiral, to whom the Earls of Essex and Southampton, kneeling, surrendered their swords.

The Lord Admiral sent his prisoners under escort to Lambeth Palace "because the night was dark, and there was no passing the bridge," but early next morning they were lodged in the Tower. The Earl of Southampton, knowing "his lady was much subject unto sudden grief and passion," managed to send a letter to her :

"Sweet heart,

"I doubt not but you shall hear ere my letter comes to you of the misfortune of your friends. Be not too apprehensive of it, for God's will must be done and what is allotted to us by destiny cannot be avoided. Believe that in this time there is nothing can so much comfort me as to think you are well and take patiently what hath happened, and, contrariwise, I shall live in torment if I find you vexed for my cause. Doubt not but that I shall do well and please yourself with the assurance that I shall ever remain your affectionate husband."

Lady Southampton, nearly distracted at the ill news, hurried up to London, but neither she nor Lady Essex could do much to help their husbands. In this hour of extremity they bewailed their youthful vanity, when as light-hearted girls they had entered into competition with a middle-aged Queen for the love of her youthful favourites. They had won, but little mattered victory now that their husbands' lives lay in the Queen's hands. In distraction, Lady Southampton appealed to Sir Robert Cecil:

"Fear to have my doings misconstrued hath hitherto made forbear to show the duty of a wife in this miserable distress of my unfortunate husband. Longer I could not, and live, suffer the sorrow I sustained in the place where I was, in not showing some effects of my infinite and faithful love unto him; therefore have I ventured hither, having no other meaning but prayers to God and humble petitions to His holy anointed, prostrate at her feet if it might be, to beg some favour, and by unfolding this my simple intention to obtain your good opinion and allowance, that my doing be not mistaken, but may move you to pity me the most miserable woman of the world by my Lord's miserable state. And in that through the heavy disfavour of her sacred Majesty unto myself, I am utterly barred from all means to perform those duties and good to him I ought to do, this being of all others my cross the most heavy, easily in your wisdom can you look into my woeful condition, which if you be pleased to

ELIZABETH VERNON, COUNTESS OF SOUTHAMPTON

Reproduced by the kind permission of the Duke of Portland, K.G., from a picture at Welbeck Abbey

do, I doubt not but you will pity me, and allow of this I do."[1]

On February 17th the Earls of Essex and Southampton appeared at Westminster Hall to answer a charge of high treason. After a trial lasting eleven hours they were found guilty and condemned to death. Watchers outside Westminster Hall knew the adverse verdict when they saw the two Earls leave the Hall preceded by the hangman carrying the axe with the head towards them. Eager runners carried the terrible news to the anxious wives who had waited through the long hours in alternate hope and fear. Now that the worst had happened, Lady Southampton with tear-blinded eyes wrote again to Cecil:

"The woeful news to me of my Lord's condemnation passed this day makes me in this my most amazed distress, address myself unto you and your virtues as being the only likely means to yield me comfort. There-fore I do beseech you and conjure you by whatsoever is dearest unto you that you will vouchsafe so much commiseration unto a most afflicted woman as to be my means unto her sacred Majesty that I may by her divine self be permitted to come to prostrate myself at her feet, to beg for mercy for my Lord. Oh! let me, I beseech you, in this my great distress move you to have this compassion of me I sue for, and in doing so you shall oblige me to acknowledge myself most bound unto you and to pray for your honour and prosperity.

[1] Hatfield MS. xi.

So kept alive only with hope to obtain mercy, I restlessly remain the most unhappy and miserable Elizabeth Southampton."[1]

Cecil promised to do what he could, though as one of the chief conspirators it would be difficult to save the Earl, still he could bid Lady Southampton hope, if only faintly, "he being penitent, and the Queen merciful."

Lady Essex was denied even this shred of comfort, for Essex, who always regarded the Secretary as his enemy, had during his trial accused Cecil of favouring the claim of the Spanish Infanta as heir to the throne. After this it could scarcely be expected that Secretary Cecil would concern himself to obtain the Earl's pardon. Lady Essex knew this, nevertheless, in the extremity of her distress she applied to him, remembering his former kindness to her:

"Sir,

"Although the answer I received from you two days since gave me small encouragement to flatter myself that any importunity I could make should be able to appease the scandal you had conceived to be given you by my unfortunate husband; yet had it not pleased God to pour upon me one affliction after another, and to add to the immeasurable sorrow of my heart so violent a sickness as I am not able of myself to stir out of my bed, I had presented unto your view the image of the unfortunate widow mentioned in the scriptures,

[1] Hatfield MS. xi.

122

and had never ceased to pester you with my complaints till you had afforded me some assurance that whatsoever respects you might depart from so much as wishing my husband's good, yet that an afflicted and woful lady should not wholly lose her labor, or return desperate of such comforts as the last year you so honorably ministered unto me in a great affliction, though differing from this in quality. As I received then such noble courtesies from you as must never be forgotten, so be persuaded, I beseech you, that whatsoever new favor you shall now be pleased to add to the old, shall so bind me to reverence of your virtues, as I will resolve to reckon myself a bankeroute until I have yielded some demonstrative testimony of the best that the honestest heart can express for the worthiest benefit.

"Honorable Sir, I know there be private causes to discourage me from moving, you hearing; yet, seeing the highest providence hath placed you in a calling most proper to be a means for my comfort, and that former experience hath taught me that you are rather inclined to do good, than to look alway to private interest; I beseech you, even for your virtue's sake, perform this noble office for me, as to join with the rest of your Lordships of the Council in presenting my humblest supplication to her Majesty.

"Dear Sir, I pray you bear with these tedious blots from her feeble hand and sad sick heart, that is stored with much thankfulness and infinite best wishes with you, who will ever rest your most beholding poor distressed servant, FRANCES ESSEX.

"Good Mr. Secretary, even as you desire of God that your own son never be made orphan by the untimely or unnatural death of his dear father, vouchsafe a relenting, to the not urging, if you may not to the hindering, of that fatal warrant for execution, which if it be once signed, I shall never wish to breathe one hour after."[1]

Essex in the Tower repented his accusation of Cecil, and the Chaplain so "ploughed up his heart," that he entreated the chief members of the Privy Council to visit him that he might ease his conscience. When they arrived at the Tower the condemned man made such ample confession, not only on his own behalf, but concerning all his confederates, that the lords of the Privy Council were seriously embarrassed. Amongst others he accused his sister, Lady Rich, of having been the mainspring of the rebellion, and that she "had a proud spirit" and must be looked to.

The Privy Councillors did not at all like these revelations about the beautiful Penelope, who had already been placed under restraint as one of the chief conspirators. The Lord Admiral in particular was highly indignant with Essex for such unchivalrous conduct to his sister, and also for placing their lordships in such an uncomfortable position, for having heard the Earl's confession they had to repeat it word for word to the Queen.

Elizabeth ordered Sir Robert Cecil and the Lord

[1] Lansdowne MSS. 88, 14.

Admiral forthwith to repair them unto my Lady Rich for the purpose of examining her straitly concerning her brother's revelations. The Lord Admiral, always Penelope's very good friend, guessed that the root of her ladyship's offence lay not so much in her having taken part in the rebellion, but in her having ensnared Lord Mountjoy's affections. In a letter to him the Lord Admiral wrote: "I think her Majesty would be most glad to see and look upon your black eyes here, so she were sure you would not look with too much respect of other black eyes."

Still ostensibly Lady Rich's offence lay in her having been one of the conspirators in the recent rebellion. Grieved and dismayed at her brother's accusations she asserted that she had been "more like a slave than a sister; which proceeded out of my exceeding love rather than his authority. What I have lost or suffered, besides her Majesty's displeasure, I will not mention; yet so strangely have I been wronged, as may well be an argument to make one despise the world, finding the smoke of envy where affection should be clearest."

As usual, Lady Rich's interrogators made out the best possible case for her: "She used herself with that modesty and wisdom, as, the report being made unto her Majesty, she was presently set at liberty, and sent unto my Lord her husband."[1]

Neither sister nor wife saw Essex again, for, though the Queen granted a reprieve to the Earl of Southampton, the Earl of Essex was executed on February 25th, 1601.

[1] *The Court of James I*, J. S. Brewer.

CHAPTER X

THE death of Essex by no means lessened the intrigues concerning the succession; rather it furthered them by opening the way for overtures from prominent people who had hitherto stayed their hands. The envoys from Scotland, who, fortunately for themselves, arrived too late to countenance the rebellion, hurried in all haste to the Court in order to congratulate the Queen on her escape. This done, they endeavoured very cautiously to find out the general feeling towards the succession.

Of the twelve possible claimants to the English throne, the two most generally favoured were King James VI of Scotland and Lady Arabella Stuart. Their claims were nicely balanced; both were descended from King Henry VII's daughter, Margaret of Scotland, James representing the elder branch and Arabella the younger. By right of seniority James had preference, but being a Scotsman, and therefore an alien, a certain section upheld that by feudal law he could not inherit English land, and that Lady Arabella, born and bred in England, should take precedence. Around these two ranged plots and counterplots.

Sir Robert Cecil had so far remained neutrally aloof,

though Lady Rich and her brother always represented him as being a bitter opponent to King James. The Scotch Ambassadors were therefore very pleasurably surprised to find him ready to accept overtures and give support to their master's claim. Before they returned home with the welcome news of having secured this powerful ally, the Ambassadors arranged for carrying on a correspondence through the medium of Lord Henry Howard,[1] a man "famous for secret insinuation." Very secret indeed it had to be, for, should word of it ever come to the Queen's ears, then King James would lose a kingdom, and Secretary Cecil his head.

King James's new friends wished to keep his favour restricted unto themselves, and in his letters Lord Henry Howard's "secret insinuations" were especially aimed to get his enemies into disrepute. In particular, being aware there were counter-plotters at Durham House—where lived Lord and Lady Raleigh—he inveighed against them with vituperation:

"You must remember also, that I gave you notice of the diabolical triplicity, that is, Cobham, Raleigh, and Northumberland,[2] that meet every day at Durham House, where Raleigh lies in consultation, which awakened all the best wits of the town out of suspicions of sundry kinds, to watch what chickens they could

[1] Second son of H. Howard, Earl of Surrey. Created Earl of Northampton 1604; d. 1614.
[2] Henry Percy, 9th Earl of Northumberland, m. Dorothy Devereux, widow of Sir T. Perrot.

hatch out of their cockatrice eggs that were daily and nightly sitten out."

Other people besides Lord Henry Howard wanted to know which claimant the "Triplicity of Hell" intended to support. At first Raleigh inclined to the idea of a republic, but, eventually, he and his friends tended towards Lady Arabella Stuart and a constitutional government.

They could not negotiate direct with Lady Arabella, for Elizabeth took good care that young lady remained in the country under the charge of her redoubtable grandmother, "Bess of Hardwick."[1] The young Countess of Shrewsbury,[2] Arabella's aunt and confidante, however, resided in London, and her growing intimacy with Lady Raleigh did not escape notice.

Lord Henry Howard considered Lady Raleigh, "a most dangerous woman and full of her father's[3] inventions," to be the brain and inspiration of the meetings at Durham House. Like Lady Rich, Lady Essex, and Lady Southampton, Lady Raleigh had committed the quite unforgivable offence of attracting the attention of one of Elizabeth's favourites. When the Queen discovered the iniquity of Elizabeth Throckmorton and Sir Walter Raleigh, she sent both favourite

[1] Elizabeth, Countess of Shrewsbury. Famous for her buildings, her quarrels, and the advancement of her children.

[2] Mary Cavendish, d. of "Bess of Hardwick."

[3] Sir Nicholas Throckmorton, 1515–1571. Diplomatist. Ambassador to France, 1560.

and Maid of Honour to the Tower, there to repent them at leisure. As usual in such cases she in time relented towards the male offender, but the Court door remained obstinately shut against Sir Walter's wife. The consequent social restriction irked a clever, ambitious woman like Elizabeth Raleigh, and "furious as Proserpina with failing of that restitution at Court which flatterie had moved her to expect," she presided over the secret meetings at Durham House, and urged on the "infernal trio."

The plotters were very considerably hampered by domestic tribulations, for Northumberland and Cobham were quite unable to control or influence their wives, who were, moreover, violent partisans of the Scotch succession. Not that the two partners in the "Triplicity of Hell" claimed any singularity in this respect; many men of lesser eminence in the State were equally afflicted:

> "Should all despair
> That have revolted wives, the tenth of mankind
> Would hang themselves."[1]

To begin with, the ladies had quarrelled, Lady Raleigh attributing her failure to obtain the Queen's pardon to Lady Kildare,[2] as Lord Cobham's wife still called herself. In hot indignation, Elizabeth Raleigh wrote to Cecil:

[1] *The Winter's Tale*, i, 2.
[2] Frances Howard, d. of Earl of Nottingham, the Lord Admiral. She married, 1st, Henry Fitzgerald, Earl of Kildare, 2nd, Henry Brooke, Lord Cobham.

"I understand it is thought by my Lady Kelldare that you should do me the favour to let me know how unfavourably she hath dealt with me to the Queen. It is true I should not have mistrusted so unhonourable a thought in her without good proof, but I protest I never understood it by you, neither did I ever see you or hear from you since her Ladyship did me that good office. I only say this that for the honour I bear her name and the ancient acquaintance of her, I wish she would be as ambitious to do good as she is apt to the contrary."

Lady Kildare, who would never under any circumstances have worked with Lady Raleigh, wrote on her own account to King James offering her "uttermost endeavour and best credit (which she maketh very great) in undertaking the disgrace of Cecil and Raleigh with the Queen." James, to the extreme annoyance of Cecil and Howard, welcomed overtures from various ladies, and replied cordially to Lady Kildare, who arranged for Dickinson, one of her servants, to be the medium for the conveyance of correspondence. Backwards and forwards to Scotland went Dickinson, to the alarm and consternation of the party at Durham House. Cobham, a weak, foolish man with no authority whatsoever over his wife, at length suggested getting the Queen to intercept Dickinson and so put an end to the correspondence by that drastic method. His friends at Durham House thought of a plan more subtle and less dangerous:

"There is a new invention among that crew, that Cobham should court his wife, and force his own disposition to make use of her access and industry, and still the Admiral, if it be possible, who now barkes at all their out ridings, and expresseth passion, though without prejudice hitherto."

If Cobham could have brought himself to follow this advice he might have found out all Lady Kildare's secrets, for her weakness for her foolish husband, combined with her own violent temper, caused the Cecil party to "clap on all our sails when she doth but offer to approach, or underhand to contraЄt with us." They knew full well, that "beside the peril of her traffic which is full of inconvenience, thus weak she is also, by strange affeЄtion to Cobham, whom never woman loved, or will love besides herself," if he would but follow his friends' advice and make pretended love to her, "he might the same instant not only descry the card, but ingress the gain unto himself, of all the voyages and discoveries which she hath made from the first day of putting to sea."

Lady Kildare would like to have had the credit of converting Sir Robert Cecil to the Scottish succession, and she paid several visits trying to find out the inscrutable Secretary's secret inclinations. Cecil proved far too clever for Lady Kildare, "for sometimes he spoke of King James with respeЄt, and afterwards, in a long time again, he would never so much as speak of him." But one day Lady Kildare received a letter from

Scotland of such unpleasing tenure, that she jumped to the conclusion that not only was Cecil in actual communication with King James, but had, moreover, written very unfavourably of herself. The violence of her rage alarmed Lord Henry Howard, who told a friend in Scotland what an anxious time they had had:

"She was in such a passion out of disdain as I assure your Lordship that if she (had) been discovered and detected to the Queen by Cobham, as for a week more the Queen's strange countenance to her, gave us all cause to fear she was resolved to have accused Cecil also, with as many probabilities as suspicion and spleen could heap together, of running the same course with King James, to the utter ruin of all her best adventures. For to my own worthy nephew the Lord Thomas Howard,[1] who is her Counsellor at these streights, she threatened to break the neck of that weasel (which was her own term) that had disgraced her."

Cecil and Lord Henry Howard having been so near the edge of the precipice, earnestly besought King James not to place them in such danger again by carrying on a correspondence with so indiscreet a woman. Surely His Majesty would perceive for himself:

"What proportion there is between the good that possibly can grow from such a busy body as understands

[1] Second son of the 4th Duke of Norfolk. Created Earl of Suffolk, 1603.

no secret of state, nor so much as ordinary passage (because her own sex dare not speak before her) and the plunge she puts the King's friends and affairs to, by these passions, upon every accident that troubles her. She is now put into the vein of seeking by good means to draw Cecil to favour King James: and here we mean to hold her, till the latter day. For I have advised Cecil, by this advantage of her intermeddling to make that impression of his respeƈt to King James which may wear out those marks which facility had left in her mind before, for I believe it, that she keepeth in her mind a large memorial of all advantages by word and aƈtion that may hold those persons in this place in awe that she would reign over."[1]

Henry, Earl of Northumberland, a man "of honourable extraƈtion and exquisite erudition," who formed the third of Lord Henry Howard's "diabolical triplicity," had a wife every wit as unmanageable as his friend Lord Cobham's. The exasperating part was that, as sister to the late Earl of Essex, Lady Northumberland was in a position to have valuable information. If she had, the very last person to hear it would be the lady's husband, for their married life had been a succession of long quarrels and short reconciliations. After an estrangement of two years' duration, they decided to live together again, but most unwisely celebrated their reunion by discussing the all-prevailing topic of the

[1] Secret correspondence of Sir R. Cecil, ed. Lord Hailes.

succession. Instantly their two hot tempers flared up; the Earl said "he had rather the King of Scots were buried than crowned, and that both he and his friends would end their lives, before her brother's great God should reign in this element."

Countess Dorothy, in a white heat of fury, replied, that "rather than any other than King James should ever reign in this place, she would rather eat their hearts in salt,[1] though she were brought to the gallows instantly." Further, she told her husband "he need not long triumph upon her poor brother's mishap, for if he kept in this mind, she could expect no better end of him than the same, or a worse destiny." With this parting taunt the Countess of Northumberland ordered her coach, bade her gentlewomen accompany her, and drove away from her husband's house.

Ten days later they made it up, chiefly because the Earl wanted an heir "to prevent the brothers that are next, whom he hates damnably, and protesteth to some of his friends, that, next his wife, he abhoreth them above any." All the same, they went on quarrelling, and Lady Dorothy's taunts so rankled in the Earl's mind, that he paid a visit to Sir Robert Cecil to complain "of his wife's Scottish heart." He thought it would be a good thing if Cecil told the Queen. This the Secretary flatly refused to do, and advised the Earl to forbear likewise, for if he should accuse his own wife "the world would abhor him." In hurting her, the

---

[1] Cf. *Beatrice:* "O God, that I were a man! I would eat his heart in the market-place." *Much Ado About Nothing*, IV, I.

Earl would hurt himself more, and Cecil advised him "to be circumspect in his passion."

Northumberland thought what Sir Robert said might be true, but, having unburdened his mind so far, he confessed to Cecil "that he had much ado to love his own daughters, because they were of that generation." Cecil endeavoured to comfort him by saying that very likely the two young ladies would take after their father and not their mother. The Earl hoped so, but doubted it; he had the poorest opinion of women, and in the general perversity of their sex, Lucy and Dorothy Percy were far more likely to grow into wilful Devereuxs like their mother and Aunt Penelope.

The conspirators at Durham House were so excessively anxious to find out if the Essex party still corresponded with Scotland, that at one of their meetings they urged the Earl to "make much of his wife for a while, to fish out the secrets of the faction of Essex." Much against his will, he agreed, with the result that Lady Dorothy, astonished at her husband's unwonted amiability, told him "the Essexians were Scottish and that the widow daily prayed for King James." He might have learnt much more by working upon "the love and kindness of a wife too good and true for him," but she received warning, and on the next occasion the Earl heard more reproaches than secrets.

Later on, after the birth of the much-desired heir, when the Earl and Countess of Northumberland were together at Syon, they discussed the succession in a more temperate manner. Undoubtedly the Queen was failing,

135

and day by day opinion hardened in favour of the King of Scotland. Even the "Triplicity of Hell" had lessened in zeal towards Lady Arabella, and were seeking to get in touch with Scotland.

The Earl of Northumberland, talking the matter over with his wife, agreed that he would rather serve a king than a queen, but objected to James on the score of his being a confirmed Protestant, whereas Lady Arabella, not being anything in particular, could be induced to favour the Catholics. Lady Dorothy suggested he should correspond with King James on the subject of religious toleration, and the Earl, acting on this suggestion, did so. James in reply promised that if the Catholics supported his claim, they should receive every consideration and be allowed liberty of conscience. Satisfied on this point, the Earl changed his political opinions, and joined the party of which his wife and her sister, Lady Rich, were two of the chief leaders.

King James's position now seemed assured, for, though Queen Elizabeth refused either to admit she was growing old or to appoint a successor, the chief men and women of the time had chosen an heir for themselves, and were in constant communication with him.

CHAPTER XI

A GREAT reign was drawing to its close; for over forty years had passed since Elizabeth ascended the throne amid the high hopes and acclamations of her people. The young girl-queen was an old woman now, but the fruits of her reign were seen on every side: a great England, great deeds, great discoveries, great men, great women—these were the laurels laid at the feet of England's Elizabeth. To her the nation had looked, almost as to a divinity in their adoration, and the virgin Queen had acted as an inspiration, typifying the ideal of chivalry. This idolization of the Queen had affected the position of women, and men vied with one another in their reverence and admiration.

Authors, poets, dramatists, were alike anxious that their works should be ushered into the world under the patronage of the famous cultured women of the day. The ladies with their deep interest in literature were ready enough to extend their patronage to men of talent, even though the office of patroness entailed certain pecuniary obligations. Some indeed were over-anxious for the honour, according to Thomas Nash, who in *Christ's Tears over Jerusalem* complained, "I hate these female braggarts that contend to have all the Muses beg at their doors."

Writers of repute were particular that their work should gain in estimation by the renown of its patron or patroness, though their needy brethren might gratify the vanity of social aspirants:

> "When we for recompense have prais'd the vile,
> It stains the glory in that happy verse
> Which aptly sings the good."[1]

Edmund Spenser, who wrote *The Faery Queen* in honour of Queen Elizabeth "to live with the eternity of her fame," dedicated many of his poems to different society ladies, celebrated for their intellectual attainments. In offering his *Four Hymnes* to the two devoted sisters, Ann, Countess of Warwick, "a lady of excellent character, and of most refined parts and education,"[2] and Margaret, Countess of Cumberland,[3] he wrote:

"Having in the greener times of my youth, composed these former two Hymnes in the praise of love and beautie, and finding that the same too much pleased those of like age and disposition, which being too vehemently carried with that kind of affection, do rather

[1] *Timon of Athens*, I, I.

[2] *Reliquiæ Wottonianæ*.

[3] Daughters of Francis Russell, second Earl of Bedford. Ann m. Ambrose Dudley, Earl of Warwick; Margaret m. George Clifford, 3rd Earl of Cumberland.

sucke out poyson to their strong passion, then hony
to their honest delight, I was moved by the one of you
two most excellent ladies, to call in the same. But being
unable so to doe, by reason that many copies thereof
were formerly scattered abroad, I resolved at least to
amend, and by way of retraction to reforme them, making
in stead of those two Hymnes of earthly or naturall love
and beautie, two others of heavenly and celestiall. The
which I doe dedicate joyntly unto you two honorable
sisters, as to the most excellent and rare ornaments of
all true love and beautie, both in the one and the
other kinde, humbly beseeching you to vouchsafe the
patronage of them, and to accepet my humble service,
in lieu of the great graces and honourable favours
which ye dayly shew unto me, untill such time as
I may by better meanes yield you some more
notable testimonie of my thankfull mind and dutifull
devotion."

To the same two sisters renowned for their "greatness
and goodness," Henry Constable indited a sonnet:

> "You sister muses doe not ye repine
> That I two sisters doe with nyne compare
> For eyther of these sacred two, more rare
> In vertue is, then all the heavenly nyne.
>
> But if ye aske which one is more devine
> I say—like to theyre own twin eyes they are
> Where eyther is as clear as clearest star
> Yet neyther doth more cleare than other's shine.

Sisters of spotless fame ! Of whom alone
Malitiouse tongues take pleasure to speake well
How should I you commend when eyther one
All things in heaven and earth so far excell.

The highest praise that I can give is this
That one of you like to the other is."

The two Countesses belonged to the generation that
was quickly passing away, for younger women with new
ideas were looking forward with scarcely concealed
impatience to the opening of a new reign when they
too might come into their own. The dignified, fine-
natured women of the Elizabethan era upheld its
traditions to the end, though passing years diminished
their numbers, and few were left like Lady Warwick who,
as maid, wife, and widow, had served the Queen for
forty years. She and her contemporaries belonged to
the old school—the truest, wisest, greatest era of
womanhood—and when they were gone the world
would not look upon their like again. Happy in their
epoch, they would never be wholly forgotten, for from
them Shakespeare drew inspiration for his heroines, the
immortal Portia, Beatrice, Rosalind, Juliet, Ophelia,
Viola, Perdita, Desdemona, Imogen, Cordelia, and
other charaĉters of Elizabethan women.

Lady Warwick, though she would not have gone to
a public theatre, saw Shakespeare's plays when they
were performed at Court before the Queen. The
Countess had a special interest in the dramatist as a
Stratford man, for, as the widow of Ambrose Dudley,
Earl of Warwick, she had inherited lands in Warwick-

LADY WARWICK

Reproduced by the kind permission of the Duke of Bedford

shire, and was Lady of the Manor of Rowington. In 1602 Shakespeare purchased a cottage and ground in Chapel Lane, Stratford-on-Avon, but, failing to comply with some formalities due to Lady Warwick as lady of the manor, the property remained in her hands till Shakespeare made a special journey into Warwickshire to rectify his error, and obtained the copyhold from her ladyship.

The closest affection existed between Lady Warwick and her youngest sister, Margaret, whose married life had turned out so unhappily. Incompatibility of temperament might have been urged in their case, for George, Earl of Cumberland, Queen's champion explorer, and man of many parts, had an "extreme love to horse-races, tiltings, boating-matches, shooting, and all such expensive sports"; whilst his wife "was truly religious, devout, and conscientious, even from childhood; and did spend much time in reading the scriptures and other good books, and in heavenly meditations, and in prayers, fastings, and deeds of charity."

With such different tastes, husband and wife could have little in common, and the Earl left her for other society. After his desertion the Countess resided chiefly with Lady Warwick at her house in the lovely garden of the dismantled Austin Friars priory in Broad Street. There the two sisters, so dearly loving each other, interested themselves in the education of Lady Cumberland's only surviving child, Ann Clifford.[1] The little

[1] 1590–1676. M. 1st, 1609, Richard Sackville, Earl of Dorset. 2nd, 1630, Philip Herbert, Earl of Pembroke.

girl repaid the love lavished upon her, and of her "dear and blessed mother" she wrote:

"She was naturally of a high spirit, though she tempered it by grace, having a very well-favoured face, with sweet and quick grey eyes, and of a comely personage. She was of a graceful behaviour, which she increased the more by being civil and courteous to all sorts of people. She had a discerning spirit both in the dispositions of human creatures and natural causes, and into the affairs of the world. She had a great, sharp, natural wit, so as there were few things worthy of knowledge but that she had some insight into them, for though she had no language but her own, there are few books of worth translated into English, but she read them, whereby that excellent mind of hers was much enriched, which even by nature was endowed with the seeds of the four moral virtues, Prudence, Justice, Fortitude, and Temperance. She was a lover of the study and practice of alchemy, by which she found out excellent medicines, and did much good to many. She delighted in distilling of waters and other chemical extractions; for she had some knowledge in most kind of minerals, herbs, flowers, and plants. She was dearly beloved by those of her friends and acquaintance that had excellent wits and were worthy and good folks; so as towards her latter end she would often say that the kindness of her friends towards her had been one of the most comfortable parts of her life."

Notwithstanding her reputation for humility, Lady

Cumberland could be obstinate enough when she chose, and proved so tenacious in asserting her own and her little daughter's rights, that a candid friend wrote and told her:

"Your lady'pp is heald to be very honorable, much devoted to religion, very respective unto ministers and preachers, very charitable to the poor; yet under favour, som do tax your honor to be too much affected to go to law."[1]

Mother and aunt devoted themselves to the upbringing of little Ann Clifford, the light of both their lives. Lady Ann, when in after years she looked back on her childhood days at Austin Friars and Clerkenwell Green, described herself as "very happy in my first constitution both in mind and in body for internal and external endowments; for never was there child more equally resembling both father and mother than myself. The colour of mine eyes were black, like my father; and the form and aspect of them was quick and lively, like my mother's. The hair of my head was brown and very thick, and so long that it reached to the calf of my legs when I stood upright; with a peak of hair on my forehead, and a dimple in my chin, like my father's; full cheeks and round face, like my mother; and an exquisite shape of body resembling my father."

Lady Cumberland took care that her daughter should have the best education possible "seasoning her youth with the grounds of true religion and morall virtue," and engaging Samuel Daniel, the well-known poet who

[1] *History of Craven*, Whitaker.

143

had been tutor to William, Earl of Pembroke, to supervise Lady Ann's studies. The Earl of Cumberland would not allow his daughter to be taught any foreign language, " but for all other knowledge befit for her sex none was bred to greater perfeftion than herself." The child proved an apt pupil, for, being always in the company of two such cultured women as her mother and aunt, she instinftively loved books, especially delighting in Montaigne's *Essays*, Gerard's *Herbal*, Sir Philip Sidney's *Arcadia, Don Quixote*, and the poetical works of Edmund Spenser and her tutor, Mr. Daniel.[1] Quick-witted, interested in all things worth knowing, Lady Ann grew up clever, accomplished, able to "discourse with virtuosos, travellers, scholars, merchants, divines, statesmen, and with good housewives, in any kind." Dr. Donne, the witty dean of St. Paul's, who was a great admirer of clever women, paid compliment to Lady Ann's versatility by saying of her that "she knew well how to discourse of all things, from predestination down to slea-silk."

Lady Cumberland took care not to overweight the little girl's mind with too much learning, considering social and domestic accomplishments of equal importance to fit her for after life. Mr. Stephens, a dancing-master, attended regularly to teach Lady Ann the latest steps, whilst a musician instrufted her how to play the virginals. It was the fashion, too, for girls interested in music to meet together, ostensibly to play

[1] Lady Ann Clifford erected monuments both to Spenser and Daniel.

or sing, but they were not always very attentive to the matter in hand:

"One Mr. Saunders, who loved music so well as he could not endure to have it interrupted with the least unseasonable noise, being at a meeting of fancy music, only for the viols and organ, where many ladyes and gentlewomen resorted, some wanton tongues could not refraine their chatt, and loud whispers sometime above the instruments. He impatient of such harsh discords as they often interposed, the lesson being ended, riseth with his viole from his seat, and soberly addressing himself towards them, 'Ladyes,' sayes he, 'this musick is not vocall, for on my knowledge these things were never made for words.' After that they had not one word to say."[1]

Amongst recently published musical works "Pammelia" was a general favourite, for in it the composers had set the sweet-toned cries of London to music. Lady Ann, seated at her virginal, could hear the itinerant sellers calling their wares, as they sought customers at the gentlefolks' houses in Broad Street and Austin Friars:

"The common cries of London Town,
Some go up street and some go down."

Many of them sounded very enticing to a small girl at her lessons: "I have ripe strawberries, ripe strawburyes"; "Fine oranges, fine lemons"; "I have fresh cheese and creame"; "Codlings, hot codlings." Vegetable sellers cried, "White unions, white St. Thomas unions"; "Radishes or lettis, two bunches a penny";

[1] Thoms's *Anecdotes and Traditions.*

"Buy my hartichokes, Mistris"; "I ha' ripe couccumber, ripe cowccumber." A woman laden with all kinds of brushes and brooms passed slowly along calling:

> "New broomes, green broomes, will you buy any?
> Come Maydens, come quickly, let me take a penny."[1]

With a keen eye for possible customers at doorways or windows, she continued her way still singing:

> "My broomes are not steeped,
> But very well bound:
> My broomes be not crooked,
> But smooth out and round.
> I wish it would please ye,
> To buy of my broome;
> Then would it well ease me,
> If market were done.
>
> Have you any olde bootes
> Or any olde shoone:
> Powch-rings or briskins,
> To cope for new broome.
> If so you have, Maydens,
> I pray you bring hether;
> That you and I friendly
> May bargen together.
>
> New broomes, new broomes, will you buy any?
> Come Maydens, come quickly, let me take a Peny."

When the broom woman had passed up Broad Street towards the City, other sellers followed in quick succession, offering every conceivable object for sale or barter. "I have screenes, if you desier, to keepe ye butey from ye fire"; "Buy a steele, or tinder-box"; "Have you

---

[1] *The Three Lords and Three Ladies of London*, 1584.

any work for a tinker?" "Buy my dish of great smelts";
"What kitchen-stuffe have you, maids?" "Buy a mouse-
trap," "Rock samphire," "A hassock for your pew,"
"New oysters"; "Have you any wood to cleave?" "Hot
peas," "Hot fine oat-cake," "Whiting, maids, whiting."

In the afternoons, when Lady Ann had finished her
lessons, she sometimes went on a shopping expedition
accompanied by a waiting-woman. The bright-eyed
girl found much to attract her in the shops as she fulfilled
the commissions entrusted to her by her mother. At
a mercer's shop at the Sign of the Holy Lamb in St.
Martin's, Lady Ann purchased some fine lawn for a ruff,
going on to a Frenchwoman for the rabato wire required
to stiffen the ruff. At another mercer's she bought a
pair of jersey stockings, and a pair of green worsted
stockings. To wear with these she required some shoes
and chose two pairs of Spanish leather and one of
calf-leather. Other purchases were some handkerchiefs,
an hour-glass, two knotts of virginal wire, some sleave
silk, two dozen glass flowers, four little pendants and
a ring, a little ivory box: nor did Lady Ann forget
two paper-covered books, one in which to keep her
accounts and "the other to write her catachiesme."

Often Lady Ann accompanied her mother to private
parties at one or other of the great houses, where the
guests were entertained by plays, masques, jugglers, and
other amusements, for there was no lack of gaiety during
the winter of 1602, though the Queen's increasing weakness alarmed Lady Warwick and those about her, and
occasioned much talk in secret concerning the succession.

CHAPTER XII

L ADY WARWICK could be little at Austin Friars, for she did not like to be much away from the Queen she had served so long, now that it was obvious to every one except herself that she could not live much longer. Had Elizabeth been younger, or Ann Clifford older, Lady Warwick would have caused her niece to be appointed one of the Maids of Honour, as she herself had been in the long, long ago when she and her mistress were merry, light-hearted girls together. Lady Ann had heard many tales of those far-off days when the world lay at the feet of England's Queen, for the younger generation could only know by hearsay of the glories of the reign now so near its close. Of the few remaining months Lady Ann Clifford kept a diary wherein she narrated the passing of the great Elizabeth, and the coming of her successor:

"In the yeare of our Lord
"1603.

"In Christmas I used to goe much to the Court, and sometymes did lye in my Aunt of Warwick's chamb^r on a pallet, to whom I was much bound for hir continuall care and love of me: in so much as if Queene Elizabeth had lived, she intended to have prefered me to be of ye privie chamber; for at that tyme ther was as much hope and expectation of me both for my person and my fortunes as of any other yeonge lady what soever.

"A little after the Queene removed to Ritchmond she began to grow sicklie: my La: used to goe often thither and caried me wth hir in the coach, and useinge to wait in the coffer chamber, and many tymes came home verie late. About the 21th or 22th of March my Aunt of Warwicke sent my mother word about 9 of ye clock at night, she lieinge then at Clerkenwell, y^t she should remove to Austen Friers hir house for feare of some comotion, thoughe God in his mercie did deliver us from it. Uppon the 24th Mr. Hocknell, my Aunt of Warwick's man, brought us word from his La: that the Queene died about ⅔ of ye clock in the morneinge. This message was delivered to my mother and me in the sâme chamber wher afterwards I was married. About 10 of the clock Kinge James was proclaimed in Cheapside by all ye Counsell wth great joy and triumphc, which triumphe I went to see and heare.

I was at Queene Eli: death 13 yeeres old and 2 moneths and this day Mr. Richard Sackville was just 14 yeeres old, he beinge then at Dorset House wth his grandfather and that great familie. At ye death of this worthy Queene my mother and I laie at Austin Friers in the same chamber wher afterwards I was married.

"This peaceable comeinge in of the Kinge was unexpected of all sorts of people. Wth in 2 or 3 daies we returned to Clerkenwell againe. A litle after this Queene Elizabeth's corps came by night in a barge from Ritch-

149

mond to Whithall, my mother and a great companie of
ladies attending it, wher it continued a good whil stand-
inge in the drawinge chamber,
wher it was watched all night
by severall Lo: and Ladies; my
mother sittinge up wth it 2 or 3
nights; but my La: would not
give me leave to watch by reason
I was heald too yeonge. At this tyme we used to goe
verie mutch to Whithall, and walked mutch in the
garden, wch was much frequented wth Lords and Ladies,
being all full of severall hopes, everie man expe&tinge
mountaines and findinge mole hills, exceptinge Sr Robert
Cicill and ye house of the Howards who hated my mother,
and did not much love my aunt of Warwicke.

The first tyme the Kinge
sent to the Lords in Eng: he
gave comaund that the Earles
of Northumberland and Cumberland the Lo: Tho. Howard
and ye Lo: Mountjoy should be
added to the Counsel.

"About this tyme my Lo: of Southampton was
enlarged of his emprisonment out of the Tower. When
the corps of Queene Elizabeth
had continued at Whithall as
longe as the Counsell had
thought fit, it was caried from thence wth great
solemnitie to Westminster, the Lords and Ladies goinge
on foot to attend it, my mother and my Aunt of Warwick
being mourners, but I was not alowed to be one because
I was not high enoughe, wch did mutch trouble me
then; but yet I stood in the church at Westminster
to se the solemnitie performed.[1]

Queene Eliz: funerall was
the 28 of April beinge Thurs-
day.

[1] "The 28 day of April, being her funerall-day, at which
time the cittie of Westminster was surcharged with multitudes
of all sorts of people in their streets, houses, windows, leads, and

"A little after this my Lady and a great deale of other companie, as Mrs. Elizab: Bridges,[1] my La: Newton and hir daughter, my La: Finch, went downe wth my Aunt of Warwick to North Hall, and from thence we all went to Tibbals to se the Kinge, who used my mother and my aunt very gratiouslie; but we all saw a great chaunge betweene the fashion of the Court as it was now, and of y[t] in y[e] Queen's, for we were all lowzy by sittinge in S[r] Thomas Erskin's chamber.

"As the Kinge came out of Scotland, when he lay at Yeorke, ther was a striffe betweene my father and my Lord Burleighe, who was then President, who should carie the sword; but it was adjuged one my father's side, because it was his office by inheritance, and so is lineally desended on me.[2]

A dispute between Geo. E. of Cumberland & the L[rd] Burleigh, about carrying the sword before the King at York, adjudged in favour of the s[d] Earl.

"From Tibballs the Kinge went to Charterhouse,

gutters, that came to see the obsequie; and when they beheld her statue or picture lying uppon the coffin set forth in royall robes, having a crowne uppon the head thereof, and a ball and scepter in either hand; there was such a generall sighing, groning, and weeping, and the like hath not beene seene or knowne in the memorie of man, neyther doth any historie mention any people, time or state, to make like lamentation for the death of their soveraygne." (Stow's *Annales*.)

[1] D. of Giles, 2nd Lord Chandos. Maid of Honour to Queen Elizabeth. M. Sir John Kennedy, a Scotch Knight, who constantly sought protection from arrest for his wife's debts.

[2] Lady Ann Clifford also became hereditary High Sheriff of Westmorland.

wher my Lo: Tho: Howard was created Earle of
Suffolke, and my Lo: Montjoy Earle of Devonshire,
thd restored my Lo: of Southampton and Essex who
stood attainted; likewise he created many Barrons,
amongst wch my unckle Russel was made Lo: Russell
of Thorney; and for Knights, they weare innuemerable.

"All this Springe I had my health verie well, not
haveinge so much as a tast of the greene sicknes. My
father used to come some tymes to us at Clerken well,
but not often; for he had at this tyme, as it weare, whollie
left my mother: yet the house was kept still at his charge.

"About this tyme my aunt of Bath and hir Lord came
to London, and brought wth them my Lo: Fitzwaren
and my cozen Frauncis Bourcher, whom I mett at
Bagshot, wher I lay all night wth my cozen Frauncis
Bourcher and Mrs. Marie Carie, wch was the first be-
ginnings of the greatnes betweene us. About 5 mile
from London ther mett them my mother, my Lo: of
Bedford and his La: my unckle Russell and much other
companie, soe that we weare in number about 300,
wch did all accompanie them to Bath House, wher they
continued most of that sommer, whether I went dailie
and visited them, and grew more inward wth my cozen
Frauncis and Mrs. Cary.

"About this tyme my Aunt of Warwick went to meete
the Queene, haveinge Mrs. Bridges wth hir, and my
[cousin] Anne Vavisor; my mother and I should have
gone wth them, but that hir horses, wch she borrowed of
Mr. Elmes and old Mr. Hickley, weare not ready; yet
I went the same night and overtooke my aunt at Ditten

Hanger, my Lady Blunt's house, wher my mother came the next day to me about noone, my aunt being gone before. Then my mother and I went on o^r jorney to overtake hir, and kild 3 horses that day wth extreamitie of heate, and came to Wrest, my Lord of Kent's house, where we found the dores shutt, and none in the house but one servaunt, who only had the keyes of the Hall, so that we weare enforced to lie in the hall all night, till towards morneinge, at wch tyme came a man and lett us into the higher roomes, wher we slept 3 or 4 howers.

"This morneinge we hasted away betyme, and came that night to Rockingham Castle, wher we overtooke my aunt of Warwick and hir companie, wher we continued a day or two wth old Sr Edward Watson and his Lady. Then we went to my La: Nedums, who once served my aunt of Warwick, and from thence to a sister of hirs whose name I have forgotten. Thither came my La: of Bedford,[1] who was then so great a woman wth the Queene as everie body much respected hir, she haveinge attended the Queene from out of Scotland.

"The next day we went to Mr. Griffin of Dinglies, wch was the first tyme I ever saw the Queene and Prince Henrie, wher she kissed us all, and used us kindly. Thither came my La: of Suffolk,[2] my yeonge La: Darby,[3]

[1] Lucy, d. of John, 1st Lord Harington, of Exon. She was famous as a patroness of poets. Ben Jonson says she had "a learned and a manly soul."

[2] Catharine, d. of Sir H. Knevit of Charlton, Wilts.

[3] Elizabeth Vere, d. of Eduard, Earl of Oxford, and Ann Cecil, Maid of Honour to Queen Elizabeth.

and my La: Walsingham, wch 3 Ladies wear the great favorits of Sr Robert Sicill. That night we went alonge wth the Queene's traine, ther beinge an infinit companie of coaches; and, as I take it, my aunt and my mother and I lay at Sr. Ritchard Knightlies, wher my La: Eliz. Knightly made exceedinglie much of us. The same night my mother and I, and my coz: Ann Vavisor rid on horseback throw Coventrie, and went to a gentleman's house wher ye La: Eliz. hir grace lay, wch was the first tyme I ever saw hir, my La: Kildare and ye La: Harington being hir governesses. The same night we returned to Sr. Ritchard Knightlies.

"The next day, as I take it, we went alonge wth the Queene to Althroppe, my Lo: Spensers house, wher my mother and I saw my Cozen Henrie Clifford, my unckle's son, wch was the first tyme we ever saw him.

"From thence ye 27, beinge Munday, the Queene went to Hatton Fermers, wher the Kinge mett hir, wher ther wear an infinit companie of Lords and La: and other people, that the countrie could scarce lodge them.

The Queene and Prince came to Althorpe the 23 of June, beinge Saterday, but as I remember my Aunt of Warwick, my mother and I, came not thither till the next day, wch Sunday was kept with great solemnitie, ther being an infinit number of Lords and Ladies. Heere we saw my coz. Clifford first. Heere we saw the Queenes favore to my La: Hatton and my La: Cicill; for she shewed noe favore to the elderly La^s: but to my La: Rich and such like companie.

"From thence the Court removed and wear banquetted wth great royaltie by my father at Grafton, wher the King and Queene weare entertayned wth speeches and delicat presents, at wch tyme my Lord

154

and the Allexanders did run a course at ye feild, wher he hurt Hen: Allexander verie dangerouslie. Where the Court lay this night I am uncertaine.

"At this tyme of the King's being at Grafton, my mother was ther, but not heald as Mrs. of the House, by reason of ye difference betweene my Lo: and hir, wch was growen to a great height.

"The night after, my aunt of Warwick, my mother, and I, as I take it, lay at Doctor Challeners (wher my aunt of Bath and my unckle Russell mett us, wch house my grandfather of Bedford used to lie much at), being in Amersom.

"The next day the Queene went to [a] gentlemans house (whose name I can not rememb^r) wher ther mett hir many great Ladies to kiss her hands; as, the Marquess of Winchest^r, my La: of Northumberland, my La: of Southampton, &c.

"From thence the Court removed to Windsor, wher the Feast of St. George was solemnised, thoughe it should have bin don before; ther I stood wth my La: Eliz: grace in the schrine in the great Hall at Windsor, to se the Kinge and all the Knights sit at dinner. Thither came the Archduk's Embassador, who was receaved by the Kinge and Queene in the great Hall, wher ther was such an infinit companie of Lo: and La: and so great a court as I think I shall never se the like. From Windsor the Court removed to Hampton Court, wher my mother

At Windsor ther was such an infinit number of Ladies sworne of the Q. privy chamber as made the place of no esteeme or credit.

Once I spake to my La: of Bedford to be one, but had the good fortune to miss it.

and I lay at Hampton Court in one of the round towers, round about wch weare tents, wher they died 2 or 3 a day of ye plague. Ther I fell extreamely sicke of a fever, so as my mother was in some doubt it might turne to the plague; but wthin 2 or 3 daies I grew reasonnable well, and was sent away to my coz: Studalls at Norburie, Mrs.

At Hampton Court, my mother, my selfe and the other Ladies dined in the presence, as they used in Queene Eliza: tyme; but that custome lasted not longe.

About this tyme my La: of Hertford[1] began to grow great wth the Q. and the Q. wore her picture.

Carington goinge wth me; for Mrs. Taylor was newly put away from me, hir husband dieinge of the plague shortly after.

"A litle afore this tyme my mother and I, my Aunt of Bath, and my cozen Frauncis went to North hall (my mother being extreame angrie wth me for rideinge before wth Mr. Meverell), wher my mother in hir anger comaunded ^{yt} I should lie in a chamber alone, wch I could not endure; but my cozen Frauncis got the key of my chamb^r and lay wth me, wch was the first tyme I loved hir so verie well.

"The next day Mr. Meverell as he went abroade fell downe suddainly and died, soe as most thought it was of the plague, which was then verie riffe. It put us all in great feare and amazement, for my aunt had then a sute to follow in court, and my mother to attend the Kinge about the busines betweene my father and hir. My aunt of Warwike sent us medicines from a litle

[1] Frances Howard, d. of Viscount Bindon, 3rd wife of Edward Seymour, Earl of Hertford.

MARGARET COUNTESS OF CUMBERIAND

Reproduced by the kind permission of the Bodleian Library, Oxford

house neare Hampton Court, wher she then lay wth Sr Moyle Finch and his La:

"Now was the Master of Orckney, and the Lord Tillebarne much in love wth Mrs. Cary, and came thither to se us, wth George Murrey in their companie, who was one of the Kinge's bed chamber. Wthin 9 or 10 daies we weare allowed to come to the Court againe, wch was before I went to my cozen Studalls.

"Uppon the 25th of July the Kinge and Queene weare crowned at Westminster; my father and my mother both attended them in their robes, my Aunt of Bathe and my unckle Russell; wch solemne sight my mother would not let me se, because the plague was so hott in London. Therefore I continued at Norburie; wher my cozen did so feed me wth breakfasts and peare pies, and such things, as shortlie after I fell into the greene sicknes.

My cozen Fran. Bourcher stood to see the coronation, though she had no robes, and went not amongst the companie.

"After the coronation the Court returned to Hampton Court, wher my mother fetched me from Norburie, and so we lay at a litle house neere Hampton Court about a fortnight, and my aunt of Bath lay in Huggens lodgins, wher my cozen Frauncis and I and Mary Cary did use to walk much about the gardens and house when the Kinge and Queene was gone.

"About this tyme my cozen Ann Vavisor was married to Sr Ritchard Warberton.

"From Hampton Court my mother, my aunt of Bath, my selfe, and all o^r companie went to Launcelevell, s^r Fra: Palmes his house, wher we continued as long as the Court lay at Bassing Stoke, and went often thither to the Queene and my La: Arbella.

"Now was my La: Ritch growen great wth the Queene, in so much as my La: of Bedford was somethinge out wth hir, and when she came to Hampton Court was entertayned but even indifferentlie, Betweene Launce levell and Mr. Dulons we lay at one Sr Edmond Fettiplaces called Besileslee, wher we had great entertaynement. Then we lay a night or 2 [at] Wantage at Gregorie Webs, a tennant of my Lo: of Bath's, and from his house to Mr. Dulons.

and yet continued to be of ye bed chamb^r. One day the Queene went from Baseinge Stoack and dined at Sr Hen: Wallups, wher my Lady, my aunt and I, had layen 2 or 3 nights before, and did healpe to entertayn hir.

"As we rid from my La: Wallups to Lance-levell, rideinge late, by reason of our stay at Basing Stoke, we saw a straunge comet in the night, like a cannopie in the aire, wch was a thinge observed over all England.

"From Lance-levell we went, as appears in the marginall note in the 9th leafe, to Mr. Dulons, wher we continued about a weeke and had great entertaynement. And at that tyme kept a fast by reason of the plague, wch was then generally observed over all England.

"From Mr. Dulons we went to Barton to one Mrs. Dormers, wher M^{rs}. Hampshire, hir mother, and she, entertayned us wth great kindnes. From thence we went often to the Court at Woodstock, wher my Aunt of Bath followed her sute to the Kinge, and my mother wroat lers to the Kinge, and hir means was by my Lo: Fenton, and to the Queene by my La: of Bedford. My father at this tyme followed hir [his] sute to ye Kinge about the border lands; so that sometymes my mother and he did meet by chaunce, wher ther countenance did shew the dislik they had one of ye other: yet he would speak to me in a slight fashion, and give me his blessinge.

"While we lay heere we rid through Oxford once or twice, but whether we went I rememb^r not. Ther we saw the Spannish Embassador, who was then new come into England about the peace. While we lay at Barton I kept so ill a diet wth Mrs. Mary Cary and Mrs. Hinson in eatinge fruit so I fell shortly after into the greene sicknes.

Not longe before Michaelmas my self, my cozen Frauncis Bour, Mrs. Goodwin & Mrs. Haukrige waiteing on us, went in my mothers coach from Barton to Cookam, wher my Unckle Russell & his wif and his son then lay. From thence ye next day we went to Nonesuch, wher Prince Henrie and hir Grace lay, wher I stayed about a week, and left my cozen Fr: ther, who was purposed to continue wth hir grace; but I came back by Cookam & came to Barton before my Aunt of Bath went into the countrie.

"From this place my Aunt of Bath, haveing little hope of hir sute, tooke hir leave of my mother, and returned into the west cuntrie. While they lay at Barton my mother and my aunt payed for the charge of the house equallie.

"Some weeke or fortnight after my aunt was gone, wch was about Michaelmas, my La: went from Barton to Greenes Norton, and lay one night at my cozen Tho: Sellengers, wher we saw old Mr. Hicklin, wher he and his daughter preferd William Pond to searve my Lady. To this place we came about 10 of ye clock in the night, and I was so wearie as I could not tell whether I should sleepe or eate first.

"The next day we went to North-hall, wher we found my Aunt of Warwick[1] something ill and melancholy; she hir selfe had not been ther passinge a moneth, but lay at S Moyle Finches in Kent, by reason of the great plague, wch was then much about North Hall.

"Not longe after Michaellmas my unckle Russell, my Aunt Russell his wife, their son, my Lo: of Bedford, my mother, and I, gave all allowance to Mr. Chambers, my Aunts Steward, in wch sort the house was kept duringe o^r being ther. I used to weare my haire-cullered velvet gowne everie day, and learned to singe and play on the bass viol of Jack Jenkins, my Aunts boye.

"Before Christmas my Cozen Frauncis was sent for from Nonesuch to North-hall, by reason that hir grace was to goe from thence to be brought up wth the La: Harington in the cuntrie. All this tyme we wear merrie at North-hall, my cozen Fra: Bourcher and my Cozen Frauncis Russell and I did use to walk much in the garden, and weare great one wth the other. At this tyme I fell directlie into the greene sicknes.

"Now ther was much talk of a maske wch the Queene had at Winchester, and how all the Ladies about the Court had gotten such ill names that it was growen a scandalous place; and the Queene hir selfe was much fallen from hir former greatnes and reputation she had in [the] world."

[1] Lady Warwick died February 3rd, 1604, and was buried at Chenies, where she left a bequest to found almshouses for ten poor widows.

CHAPTER XIII

ON his accession to the throne, King James testified his regard for those ladies who had corresponded with him during the late reign, showing especial favour to the two sisters of the late Earl of Essex, Lady Rich and Lady Northumberland, who having been in obscurity since their brother's rebellion, gladly welcomed the advent of a new reign which enabled them to take their places once more as leaders of society.

It was probably owing to his wife's position that the Earl of Northumberland received Court favour, and escaped the fate which overtook his old confederates of the "Triplicity of Hell." Raleigh and Cobham both offered service to the new King, but James, whose mind had been poisoned against them, received their overtures very coldly, and they were shortly afterwards arrested in connection with the Main plot to place Lady Arabella Stuart on the throne.

The trial took place at Winchester, when the prisoners, though found guilty and condemned to death, were reprieved at the last moment and sent to the Tower. Lady Raleigh, thankful in so much that her husband's head still remained on his shoulders, sought and obtained permission to share Sir Walter's imprisonment, from whence she constantly besought King James for some mitigation of Sir Walter's sentence.[1]

To those in Court favour, life represented an endless round of gaiety, for when the plague had abated sufficiently for the King and Queen to come to London the season opened with a round of festivities. Tradesmen shared in the general buoyancy, filling their shops with new goods over which nimble-tongued apprentices kept watch, crying, "What d'ye lack, gentlewomen, what d'ye lack, gentlewomen?" as the ladies passed along the narrow streets, looking up at the signboards which designated the different shops. Few women could pass the sign of "The White Bear" in Cheapside where Mr. Hicks,[2] the famous silk merchant, displayed his wares; cloth of gold and silver tissue, silk grograms, silver chamletts, silver tabynes, tuff taffetas, tinselled taffetas, china silk, naples silk, genoa velvets, branched satins, gold chamblets, and nets wrought with gold and silver. Such goods required long purses, for the ladies vied to outdo each other in "extreme daubing on of cost," so

[1] Raleigh remained a prisoner till 1616, when James released him to undertake an expedition to the Orinoco in search of gold. Imprisoned on his return, and executed October 29th, 1618. Cobham after several years was allowed to escape from the Tower. Lady Kildare would have nothing to do with her husband, and he died in poverty in 1619.

[2] Baptist Hicks, 1st Viscount Campden (1551–1629), made a fortune by supplying the Court with silks. Created baronet, 1620; Viscount Campden, 1628.

that people who were not drapers, milliners, silk merchants, silversmiths, tailors, cloth workers, or haberdashers, said

"the city woman bears
The cost of princes on unworthy shoulders."[1]

At a Court wedding when the minister rose to make exhortation, he did not extol the virtues of bride and bridegroom, nor give precepts for their future guidance, but turning a baleful eye upon the wedding guests, assembled in full force and in great finery, he announced a text from Proverbs, likening women to ships: "She is like a merchant's ship, she bringeth food from afar."

"But of all qualities, a woman must not have one quality of a ship and that is too *much rigging.* Oh! what a wonder it is to see a ship under full sail, with her tacklings and her masts, and her tops, and top gallants, with her upper decks and her nether decks, and so bedeckt with her streamers, flags, and ensigns, and I know not what: yea what a world of wonders it is to see a woman created in God's image, so miscreate oft times with her French, her Spanish, and her foolish fashions, that He that made her, when He looks upon her shall hardly know her, with her plumes, her fannes, and a silken vizard, with a ruffle like a saile, yea a ruffle like a *Raine-bow,* with a feather in her cap like a flag in her top, to tell (I think) which way the wind will blow."

[1] *As You Like It,* II, 7.

The sermon had a topical touch, for feathers and coloured ruffs were both bones of contention. To begin with, men, considering feathers in hats to be a masculine prerogative, resented women's attempt "to counterfaite this jolly feather," on the score of sex unsuitability, "For it hath some show of valiant courage in capitaines and lusty souldiers, but in women it smelleth somewhat of vanitie."

The ladies considered this no reason at all, and continued to flaunt feathers in their hats; nor were they to be turned aside from the prevailing craze for yellow ruffs, though their liege Majesty said quite unprintable things about saffron dyed ruffs, and the ladies who wore them. King James had all the zeal to act as an arbitrator of fashion, but found with chagrin that in this respect his new subjects would pay him no attention whatsoever. James hated the huge hooped farthingales ladies wore to make their dresses stand out, and complained that this "impertinent garment" took up all the room in his court. His dislike intensified after a masque performed for his amusement by the gentlemen of Gray's Inn, for in their anxiety to obtain good seats the ladies hurried forward, and, their dresses being large and the passage narrow, they became wedged together.

> "No man living
> Could say, 'This is my wife,' there; all were woven
> So strangely in one piece."[1]

Next morning, in a highly indignant frame of mind,

[1] *King Henry VIII*, iv, i.

164

King James issued a proclamation saying that henceforward no more farthingales were to be worn at Court. King and courtiers thought that ended farthingales; but no, smiling sweetly, ladies in enormous farthingales, and with yellow ruffs round their necks, continued to curtsy in mock obedience to their King.

Royal disapproval proved equally ineffective in the case of smoking. King James hated "the most divine tobacco," but in his new kingdom he found it "an herb so generally received in the courts of princes, the chambers of nobles, the bowers of sweet ladies, the cabins of soldiers."[1] King James took up his royal pen and wrote *A Counterblast to Tobacco*, saying, "You are not able to walk or ride the journey of a Jew's sabbath but you must have a reeky coal brought to light your pipe." Moreover, a lady "cannot in a more mannerly kind entertain her lover than by giving him out of her fair hand a pipe of tobacco." If she condescended to try his tobacco and commended it, the gentleman would feel himself highly honoured, and boast about it afterwards:

"A lady took a pipefull or two at my hands, and praised it, for the heavens."[2]

Sir Walter Raleigh introduced tobacco into polite society, and the ladies at first affected to be horrified, but desirous to do everything men did, and fortified by their doctors, who were inclined to prescribe the

[1] *Every Man in his Humour*, Ben Jonson.
[2] *Untrussing the Humorous Poet*, Dekker.

newly discovered tobacco as a cure for all ills, they were soon every whit as keen as their menfolk to come "up every term to learn to take tobacco."[1] Professors instructed novices in the new art, and so many were their clients of both sexes that, notwithstanding King James's "counterblast," there were in London seven thousand shops that sold tobacco. Apothecaries and grocers kept it as part of their stock, but critical ladies bought their supplies from a regular "tobacco-man" who did not "sophisticate" the best Virginian,

> "But keeps it in fine lily pots, that opened,
> Smell like conserve of roses, or French beans.
> He has his maple block, his silver tongs,
> Winchester pipes, and fire of juniper."[2]

The ladies, once having taken to smoking, found such solace in their long-stemmed pipes with carved silver bowls that non-smokers, wishing to be offensive, said accusingly,

> "Sister, i'faith you take too much tobacco,
> It makes you black within as you are without."[3]

King and social reformers alike might as well have spared their breath for all the notice the ladies took of them and their strictures. After two years they had taken accurate measure of their James foot, and defied him in a way they durst not have done to Queen Elizabeth.

[1] *Every Man out of his Humour*, Ben Jonson.
[2] *The Alchemist*, Ben Jonson.
[3] *The Case is Altered*, Ben Jonson.

LADY SMOKING

Reproduced from a volume by the kind permission of the Bodleian Library, Oxford

In the autumn of 1605 society ladies were in town in full force, one and all being deeply concerned over the details of the dresses they intended to wear when the King opened Parliament on November 5th. The Countess of Northumberland, always "very gallant" in her dress, was in residence at Essex House, which her husband now rented, but the Earl, who expected a visit from his cousin, Thomas Percy, manager of his estates in the North, did not leave Syon till November 4th, arriving in town so late that he went straight to bed.

Many important people got no sleep at all that night, consequent on a warning that the Papists had formed a plot to blow up the Houses of Parliament next day. Examination of the cellars resulted in the discovery of Thomas Percy's servant, Guy Fawkes, keeping watch over thirty-six barrels of gunpowder.

The Lords of the Council deputed the Earl of Worcester to go and examine Thomas Percy's cousin, the Earl of Northumberland, and find out how much he knew of the gunpowder plot. The Earl of Worcester thundered on the door of Essex House at dawn, demanding immediate admittance. Frightened servants knew not what to do, but Lord Worcester would not be denied, and upstairs he went to the Earl of Northumberland's chamber, awakened and cross-questioned him. The Earl replied "with scorn and confidence," but his assertion of innocence proved no avail, for he was deprived of all his offices, fined £30,000, and sentenced to life imprisonment in the Tower.

Lady Northumberland stood by her husband in his trouble to an extent no one who knew of their domestic quarrels would have expected. Impulsive, quick-tempered Dorothy proved untiring in her efforts to obtain the Earl's release, attacking those she considered his enemies with an outspokenness which caused them to fly at her approach. Having formed a highly unfavourable opinion of Cecil, now Earl of Salisbury, she determined to let him know it, and drove off to Whitehall with avowed intention "to give the Ferrett a nipp."

Lady Northumberland spied Salisbury walking with friends in the palace orchard, and there and then, in the presence of onlookers, did she roundly rate him, telling him either to abate her husband's fine or else come out into the open as his enemy. In vain did Salisbury strive to stay the lady's torrent of words, but having worked herself up into a passion Lady Dorothy was not to be silenced "by any Cyssle borne." Salisbury bore it as long as he could, then incontinently he fled, going home to write a complaint to Northumberland of his wife's conduct, and giving stringent orders that never under any pretext should the Countess of Northumberland be admitted to his presence again.

King James fared little better at the Countess's hands, for she did not scruple to tell him she knew very well that the true cause of her husband's imprisonment lay in the King's lack of funds, "and God forbidd that one or two poor creatures should suffer, because your ma^{ties} coffers are emptie."

Eye - witnesses, gossips, and newsmongers repeated with zeal how King and Minister had been baited by my lady, so that audiences at the Globe Theatre would doubtless applaud a topical allusion, when in *The Winter's Tale* Leontes exclaims apprehensively at seeing the outspoken Paulina advance towards him:

> "How!
> Away with that audacious lady! Antigonus,
> I charg'd thee that she should not come about me:
> I knew she would."[1]

The Countess expected the Earl to be properly appreciative of her efforts on his behalf, whereas he took up the attitude that she had "not out runne the Dutye off a wife and woman of Honor." "Shee, I confesse hath sorrowed and laboured much for theis my troubles; for the sorrowe shee had reason; and for the labour I have heard off it so often." If friends urged Dorothy's praises, her husband agreed politely, but also very guardedly and with reservations: "Iff you say shee is a worthy Lady, so say I too, and that their are her betters and Equalles, and her Inferiors, very worthy ladies." For the flaws in his wife's character Northumberland considered "over conceipt and over prising herself is the original cause"; aggravated by being "very Passionate and subiet unto her Will."

The Earl always laboured under the impression that his wife wanted to manage him, the very thought of which reduced him to a state of obstinacy when he

---

[1] *The Winter's Tale*, ii, 3.

would deliberately go against his own interests, because "it is against the nature of a man, either to be threatened or putt straight by his wife, which in me can nott, neither ever will have good effect; and in this time of my Troubles, it will but discover an insulting nature in her."

The question of a suitable allowance occasioned much heat, the Earl holding "the Difference very great betweene the Countess of Northumberland, her husband being in prison, and the Countess of Northumberland, her husband being out of prison." No amount of reasoning could make the Countess accept this point of view; so long as she remained out of prison—and she had no intention of emulating Lady Raleigh's devotion by residing in the Tower with her lord—she saw no reason whatsoever to curtail expenditure.

Extravagant in dress she always had been, and always meant to be, but now, being in possession of Syon House, she developed all sorts of fantastical notions which had never even entered the heads of former Countesses. For one thing, she insisted on having a bathroom opening out of her own bedroom, and in face of determined opposition from her imprisoned husband, she got it, and others, he having to foot the bill reluctantly.

"It cost me £400 this last year paste in building off Bathing Houses, cabinettes, and other things shee had a fancy to, which this 15 yeare before was never miste nor wanting."

The two daughters, Lucy[1] and Dorothy,[2] proved another cause of friction, for the Earl heard such accounts of the frivolity and lack of decorum at Anne of Denmark's Court that he wished to prevent the girls going there at all, telling Lady Lucy "that he was a Percy, and could not endure that his daughter should *dance any Scottish jigs.*" Lucy and Dorothy, who had fulfilled the Earl's apprehensions by growing up beautiful and wilful like all the Devereux women, paid little heed to his admonitions, for with Lord father safely under lock and key in the Tower, and Lady mother entirely of their own way of thinking, they entered into all the social gaiety of the day.

Lucy, "a lady of incomparable beauty, solemnized in the poems of the most exquisite wits of the time," became one of the reigning toasts of the day, in whose honour young men sang Ben Jonson's popular song:

> "Drink to me only with thine eyes,
>   And I will pledge with mine;
> Or leave a kiss but in the cup,
>   And I'll not look for wine.
> The thirst that from the soul doth rise,
>   Doth ask a drink divine:
> But might I of Jove's nectar sup,
>   I would not change for thine.

---

[1] Lucy, m. James Hay, 1st Earl of Carlisle, 1617. She attained celebrity during the Civil Wars; d. 1660.

[2] Dorothy, m. Robert Sidney, 2nd Earl of Leicester, 1616; Lady Sidney's son, who arrived in the world so full of measles.

I sent thee late a rosie wreath,
    Not so much honouring thee,
As giving it a hope, that there
    It could not withered be.
But thou thereon didst only breathe,
    And sent'st it back to me:
Since when it grows and smells, I swear,
    Not of itself but thee."

Meanwhile in the Tower, the Earl of Northumberland, being quite unable to control his wife and daughters, employed himself by writing a treatise on the Management of Women for the benefit of his son when he came to man's estate. Should he be so unfortunate as to be the father of daughters, he would be well advised not to devote much time or money on their education, for "the wiser the waywarder."[1] Knowing little, it was possible, though not probable, they might look up to their husbands. In order to get them off his hands as soon as possible, a father should "fashion them modest, neate, gracefull, obedient, to draw on the lykings of husbands, whereby fathers may put them off and provide them fortuns during the rest of there lyfes, that must be gott either when they are yonge or never; for then are they the prittyest; in not leaving them to worke out there own preferrements by other endevors, as by learning, the sworde, and other vertues of this nature."

If daughters showed any inclination for needlework, they should be encouraged:

[1] *As You Like It*, IV, I.

172

"To beginne great workes that will ever be in the beginning and never ended, with a littel wasting of sleave silke, for these pastimes I hold very necessary; and soe perhaps in two or three ages a bed imbrodered with slipps may be finished; or, in somme less tyme, a purse or a paire of hangers[1] wrought by her owen hand, for a servant[2] may be ended; but I have ever found that empty purses are fitter for there care than full ones."

Unfortunately, it was more likely they would be contemptuous of needlework and want to manage their husbands' estates, "the motive that spurs them to the desier of being masters." Many husbands gave in for quietness' sake, whereas they should rather pluck up courage and remember that women's only weapon is "the sharpenes of there tongues, for they can nether strike nor byte to any purpose." Of course, if they do not get their own way "they will be froward and perverse in their carriage," but "the paine is very smaule to lett an unreasonable woman sitt still and be angry without a cause," though "they doe talke preposterously," on purpose to madden their long-suffering husbands. "Revenge by way of hurt is more manly than comendable," and it is better to sit quiet till "women have chid themselves out of breathe."

Lord Percy was advised that "arguing to them what is good to be donne" is sheer waste of breath; whatever happens, women follow the fashion, and it will always be "sutche and sutche wears this or that; not what is

[1] Belts for rapiers.   [2] The professed lover.

proper for them to give, but sutche and sucche gives this and that;—not that painting is an unmodest ornament, but that painting is the fashion."

Trouble over the children surely there will be, "for wyffes will have there wills, and will believe better of there own ways then of yours, and sorry will they be to see there owen faults told them by an austere father every houre in there daughters."

Recalling scenes with the Countess, arising not unlikely from his telling her faults through the medium of Lucy and Dorothy, the Earl counselled his son not to pay much attention to women's threats.

"I have understood them to be soe violent somtymes, when they could not have there wills, as to threaten to act many mischiefs upon their owen persons; which skilfull men in this trade of there humors have remedyed by offering furtherances to ther threats; as, if they would needs kill them selves, to give them a knife; if to hang themselves, to lend them your garters; if to cast them selves headlong out of windoes, to open the casements; if to swound and dye, to lett them lye till they come to themselves againe: soe as to this day I could never here of any that perished by these mornefull deaths."[1]

The Earl of Northumberland[2] considered present-day

[1] *Archæologia*, xxvii.

[2] Northumberland remained in prison till 1621. The Countess died in 1619, when he took her loss so much to heart that his friends found it necessary "to remind the Earl of his former disputes with his wife," in order to lessen his grief at her loss.

treatment of women occasioned all the trouble, for a passionate woman will pride herself on being "a lady of good spirit," whereas in the good old days, before women were so highly educated, she would have been plainly accounted a "scold." Things might be remedied if husbands, instead of "with dalliances and attendances to be ridiculously obsequious" to their wives, asserted their authority, and in public carried "a graver and commanding fashion" towards their better halves.

CHAPTER XIV

IT would greatly have cheered the Duke of Northumberland's imprisonment had he known that already women's Star of Ascendancy was on the wane. Queen Elizabeth, by her own dominant personality, had raised the status of her sex to an unprecedented height, herself typifying the one ideal woman at whose shrine all men worshipped, she had exacted reverence, adoration, and obedience from her subjects. Society women took their pattern from the Queen, at whose virgin Court they wielded great power, and occupied many positions usually discharged by men.

King James had been fully alive to English women's importance so long as he remained in Scotland, and gladly utilized their services to secure his accession, but, once seated on the throne of England, he had no intention whatsoever of allowing women to meddle any longer in State affairs. Men favourites might twiddle him round their little fingers, but he became as obstinate as the Earl of Northumberland if he suspected women were trying to manage him. James disliked the sex both individually and collectively, but, as a choice of two evils, preferred an ignorant woman to a wise one, as being less dangerous. When a "learned Maid," who could speak and write pure Latin, Greek, and Hebrew, was presented to King James he listened unmoved to the catalogue of her attainments, merely asking dourly, "But can she spin?"[1]

King James might endeavour to debar women from political importance, and thrust them into the background, but it by no means followed they were willing to remain there. Considering what an important part this sex had played in Court intrigue during the previous reign, the present generation was excessively chagrined to find itself of no particular account now that a King, not a Queen, ruled the country. A society lady might enter with zest into all the frivolous amusements of the day, but she had other ambitions which took toll of her husband's money-bags: "If learned, there was never such a parrot; all your patrimony will be too little for the guests that must be invited to hear her speak Latin and Greek." Also she desired to be "a stateswoman, know all the news, what was done at Salisbury, what at the Bath, what at Court, what progress;[2] or so she may censure poets, and authors, and styles, and compare them; Daniel with Spenser, Jonson with the t'other youth, and so forth: or be thought cunning in controversies, or the very knots of divinity; and have often in her mouth the state of the question; andthen skip tothe mathematicsand demonstration; and answer, in religion to one, in state to another."[3]

[1] Thoms's *Anecdotes and Traditions.*
[2] When the King and Court were visiting in the country.
[3] *The Silent Woman,* Ben Jonson.

In order to discuss these subjects, the ladies decided to form a club or college of their own, after the fashion of the famous Mermaid[1] Club which refused to admit women to its gatherings. The innovation caused a good deal of talk, and occasioned a topical allusion in Ben Jonson's play, *The Silent Woman*:

"A new foundation, sir, here in the town, of ladies, that call themselves the collegiates, an order between courtiers and country-madams, that live from their husbands; and give entertainments to all the wits and braveries, of the time, as they call them: cry down, or up, what they like or dislike in a brain or a fashion, with most masculine, or rather hermaphroditical authority; and every day gain to their college some new probationer."

A fashionable lady prided herself upon her versatility and the dexterity with which she could turn from one subject to another:

"I have a little studied physic; but now
I'm all for music, save in the forenoons,
An hour or two for painting. I would have
A lady, indeed, to have all letters and arts,
Be able to discourse, to write, to paint,
But principal, as Plato holds, your music."[2]

Mary, Countess of Shrewsbury, one of the most intellectual women of the time, testified her genuine interest in learning and progress by benefactions to

[1] The *Apollo* Club, founded a few years later, admitted women as well as men.

[2] "The Fox," B. Jonson.

178

St. John's College, Cambridge, and subscriptions to the Virginian Company,[1] which aimed at establishing a new world in America.

Thomas Lodge, in a dedication to Lady Shrewsbury, wrote: "The iudgement of my industry relyeth on your Ladishippe, who haue both authoritie to conuict, and knowledge to commend. I haue chosen you Madam amongst many, to be the Soueraigne and shee *Mecænas* of my toyle, because I am assured, that the great report of your learning and vertue (wherewith as yet it hath not pleased you to dignifie the world) must euen now be exemplified in mee."

A daughter of the famous "Bess of Hardwick," Mary, Countess of Shrewsbury, had inherited a good deal of her mother's strong will. This frequently brought her into conflict with her father-in-law, George, Earl of Shrewsbury, who accused her of having a predominate influence over his son. When Gilbert[2] requested a larger allowance, his father returned "a short answer," saying, "Provide for yourself, as you may, or else be disappointed; for during my life, I would not have you to expect any more at my hands than I have already allowed you, wherof I know you might live well, and clear from danger of any, as I did, if you had that governance over your wife, as her pomp and court like manner of life were some deal assuaged, for mine own

[1] Other subscribers included Margaret, Countess of Cumberland; Lucy, Countess of Bedford; Mary, Countess of Pembroke.

[2] Gilbert Talbot, 1553–1616, 7th Earl of Shrewsbury; m. Mary Cavendish, d. of " Bess of Hardwick " by a former husband.

part, and your good, I do wish you had half so much to relieve your necessities as she and her mother have spent in seeking, through malice, mine overthrow and dishonour."[1]

Notwithstanding the advice he gave his son, George, Earl of Shrewsbury, could not put his own precepts into practice, and being quite unable to control his own wife, requested Sir Robert Cecil to punish her for him, and so strike a blow for all harassed husbands: "Good Mr. Secretary, I seek nothing but justice; and in honour it ought not to be denied me in such a cause, which, if it should go unpunished, the example were too perilous, for it may encourage other strong-hearted women to do the like; from which God deliver all good men."

Gilbert, who succeeded his father in 1590, pursued the line of least resistance, for though called "the great and glorious Earl of Shrewsbury," from the pomp in which he lived, Sir Francis Bacon told King James there was *"a greater than he, which is my Lady of Shrewsbury."*

Whatever his methods, the new Earl led a far happier married life than his father had done, for the Countess could be the staunchest friend and the most relentless enemy. She never did anything half-heartedly, even taking upon herself to avenge her husband's quarrels, so that when Sir Thomas Stanhope defaced the Earl's coat of arms on an inn sign at Newark, it was the Countess who promptly sent word that he was a rascal; his son John a reprobate; and the child yet to be con-

[1] Lodge's *Illustration*, ii.

ceived should rue what they had done. This proved merely a preliminary intimation, for the Countess, in a white heat of rage, composed a speech which she caused one of her servants to learn by heart. When he had perfected it, she bade him go forthwith and recite it, word for word, to Sir Thomas Stanhope.

"My Lady hath commanded me to say thus much to you. That, though you be more wretched, vile, and miserable than any creature living; and, for your wickedness, become more ugly in shape than any creature in the world; and one to whom none of reputation would vouchsafe to send any message; yet she hath thought good to send thus much to you:—That she be contented you should live, and doth no ways wish you death; but to this end, that all the plagues and miseries that may befall any man may light upon such a caitiff as you are, and that you should live to have all your friends forsake you; and without your great repentance, which she looketh not for, because your life hath been so bad, you will be damned perpetually in hell fire."[1]

The astounded Sir Thomas requested the messenger to repeat what he had said, but this he refused to do, volunteering the information that "if he had failed in anything, it was in speaking it more mildly, and not in terms of such disdain as he was commanded."

The Stanhopes knew the hard side of the Countess, but her niece, Lady Arabella Stuart, found her the kindest, truest friend she had in the world. King James

[1] Sloane MS. 4161.

had been very apprehensive of Lady Arabella's claims, but when he found she made no attempt to pose as his rival he invited her to Court, where she took precedence as the second lady in the land.

Arabella belonged to the old school of highly educated women, speaking Latin, Italian, French, and Spanish with fluency, whilst for relaxation she read Greek and Hebrew, and was "constantly studying." With these studious tastes she found the frivolous and childish amusements of Queen Anne's Court little to her liking, and looked forward to her Aunt Mary's letters as the greatest pleasure in her life.

"For if I should not prefer the reading of your kind and most welcome letters before all Court delights (admit I delighted as much in them as others do), it were a sign of extreme folly; and liking Court sports no better than I do, and than I think you think I do, I know you cannot think me so transformed as to esteem anything less than them. As your love and judgment together makes me hope you know I can like nor love nothing better than the love and kindness of so honourable friends as you and my uncle."

In another letter Lady Arabella told her uncle and aunt how the new Queen passed her evenings. "Whilst I was at Winchester there were certain child's plays remembered by the fair ladies, viz., 'I pray, my lord, give me a course in your parke'; 'Rise, pig, and go'; 'One penny, follow me,' etc.: And when I came to Court, they were as highly in request as ever cracking of nuts was.

So I was by the Mistress of the revels, not only compelled to play at I knew not what (for till that day I never heard of a play called 'Fier'), but even persuaded by the princely example I saw to play the child again. This exercise is most used from ten of the clock at night till two or three in the morning, but that day I made one it began at twilight and ended at supper-time."

When in town, King James resided at Whitehall, and Queen Anne at Somerset House in the Strand, her Court "being a continued maskardo, where she and her ladies, like so many sea-nymphs, or nereides, appear'd often in various dresses, to the ravishment of Beholders. The King himself not being a little delighted with such fluent elegancies as made the nights more glorious than the day."[1]

Theatricals were Queen Anne's especial delight, and soon Queen Elizabeth's gorgeous wardrobe was being cut up to make fancy dresses, whilst Ben Jonson and Inigo Jones were called upon to supply words and scenery for Court masques.

In the *Masque of Blackness*, the Queen and her ladies represented twelve negresses on a visit to England in search of a wash to whiten their complexions. According to Ben Jonson's stage directions:

"The Masquers were placed in a great concave shell, like mother of pearl, curiously made to move on those waters, and rise with the billow; the top thereof was struck with a chevron of lights, which indented to the

[1] *The Court of James I.*

183

proportion of the shell, struck a glorious beam upon them, as they were seated one above another; so that they were all seen, but in an extravagant order."

The distinguished audience which witnessed the performance was not wholly appreciative, considering that blackened faces and arms became the ladies "nothing as well as their own red and white," but rather resembled "a troop of lean-cheeked Moors"; the whole effect being "rich but too light and courtezan like for such great ones." The cost of these masques was enormous; one lady of no great social rank wearing jewels valued at over a hundred thousand pounds, "and the Lady Arabella goes beyond her; and the Queen must not come behind."[1]

Bitter were the lamentations of impoverished husbands whose wives were gratified by invitations to Court festivities, "where she must have that rich gown for such a great day; a new one for the next; a richer for the third; be served in silver; have the chamber filled with a succession of grooms, footmen, ushers, and other messengers; besides embroiderers, jewellers, tire-women, sempsters, feathermen, perfumers; whilst she feels not how the land drops away, nor the acres melt; nor foresees the change, when the mercer has your woods for her velvets."[2]

Led on by the Queen, society women entered on a phase of extravagant frivolity, throwing aside all state

[1] Letter from John Chamberlain to Sir Dudley Carleton.
[2] *The Silent Woman*, ii, i, Ben Jonson.

and decorum, till sedate folk, who could remember how different Queen Elizabeth's Court had been, were aghast at what they saw and heard. Sir John Harington,[1] the late Queen's godson, wrote to tell a friend what changes had taken place:

"I have much marvelled at these strange pageantries, and they do bring to my remembrance what passed of this sort in our Queen's days; of which I was sometimes an humble presenter and assistant: but I did ne'er see such lack of good order, discretion, and sobriety, as I have now done. I have passed much time in seeing the royal sports of hunting and hawking, where the manners were such as made me devise the beasts were pursuing the sober creation, and not man in quest of exercise or food. I will now in good sooth declare to you, who will not blab, that the gunpowder fight is got out of all our heads, and we are going on hereabouts as if the devil was contriving every man should blow up himself, by wild riot, excess, and devastation of time and temperance.

"The great ladies go well masked, and indeed it be the only show of their modesty to conceal their countenance; but, alack, they meet with such countenance to uphold their strange doings, that I marvel not at ought that happens. . . .

"If you would wish to see how folly doth grow, come up quickly; otherwise stay where you are, and meditate on

---

[1] Sir J. Harington, 1561–1612; translated *Orlando Furioso* and author of several original works.

the future mischiefs of those our posterity, who shall learn the good lessons and examples held forth in these days."[1]

After five or six years of Court gaiety, Lady Arabella Stuart was heartily weary of it all, and longed for a home of her own, but James—like his predecessor, Queen Elizabeth—thought her claims would be strengthened by marriage; therefore he made no haste to secure his cousin a suitable husband. But the years were passing, and at thirty-five Lady Arabella, with the furtherance of her aunt, Lady Shrewsbury, decided to choose for herself, and her choice fell on the one man of all others most likely to annoy King James. This was Mr. William Seymour, aged twenty-two, grandson of Lady Catherine Grey, whose clandestine marriage with the Earl of Hertford had caused such a sensation in the last reign. Elizabeth had caused Lady Catherine's children to be declared illegitimate, but, notwithstanding, a large following in the country considered their line the rightful one. Therefore when in 1610 James heard a rumour coupling the names of Lady Arabella and William Seymour, he was greatly perturbed, and caused them to be called before the Privy Council and straitly examined. So flatly did they both deny the accusation that they were liberated, when the first use they made of their liberty was to get married in right good earnest. King James, learning what had happened, promptly sent the bridegroom to the Tower and the bride into private custody at Lambeth.

[1] Harington's *Nugæ Antiquæ*.

Lady Shrewsbury, as soon as she heard what ill hap had befallen her niece, did everything possible to try and obtain her release, but failed, and Lady Arabella was ordered to proceed northward, the Bishop of Durham having been appointed her keeper. Lady Shrewsbury did not lose heart on hearing this, and by means of a confidential servant—"that trusty rogue Crompton"—managed to communicate with her niece, outlining a plan of escape. The prospect put heart into Lady Arabella, who on plea of illness received permission to halt awhile at Highgate, where Lady Shrewsbury sent her large sums of money, and a suit of man's clothes, which Crompton contrived to smuggle into the house.

All now depended on Lady Arabella's ability to counterfeit a man. As a constant spectator at Court performances of William Shakespeare's famous plays, she had had many opportunities of seeing this disguise assumed by women; but stage and real life were two very different matters. Crompton, like the servant in *Cymbeline*, could give his mistress sage advice on assuming masculine deportment:

> "Well, then, here's the point:
> You must forget to be a woman; change
> Command into obedience; fear and niceness[1]—
> The handmaids of all women, or more truly
> Woman it pretty self—into a waggish courage;
> Ready in gibes, quick-answer'd, saucy, and
> As quarrelous as the weasel."[2]

Like Imogen in the tragedy, Arabella expressed herself

[1] Wilfulness.   [2] *Cymbeline*, III, 4.

ready to make the attempt "though peril to my modesty, nor death on 't, I would adventure," and talking things over with trusty Crompton felt "almost a man already." Taking the disguise upstairs to her bedroom, Lady Arabella transformed herself into a comely youth, "by drawing a pair of great French-fashioned hose over her petticoats, putting on a man's doublet, a manlike perugue, with long locks, over her hair, a black cloak, russet boots with red tops, and a rapier by her side."

Thus, with "a swashing and a martial outside," Lady Arabella walked boldly out of the house towards the inn a mile and a half off, where Crompton awaited with the horses. By the time she reached her destination, Lady Arabella was ready to confess, like Rosalind in *As You Like It*, that "though I am caparison'd like a man," I have not "a doublet and hose in my disposition," and "could find it in my heart to disgrace my man's apparel and to cry like a woman."

The ostler who held the stirrup for the supposed young gentleman to mount remarked that he looked so ill he would hardly hold out to London, but once astride the horse Lady Arabella's spirits revived and she rode forward with good courage. At first all seemed well, for Lady Shrewsbury had laid her plans carefully, and there was a boat waiting at London to convey Arabella and her party down to Lee, where a French ship had been chartered to convey the fugitives across to the Continent. Unfortunately William Seymour, who had managed to escape from the Tower, did not arrive in time, and greatly to Arabella's distress she and her friends had to put out to sea without him.

Meanwhile the lovers' escape had been discovered, filling James with "fearful imaginations," which were not allayed till he heard that Lady Arabella had been recaptured, though her husband had managed to reach Ostend in safety.

Lady Arabella, broken-hearted over her shattered romance, and wholly innocent of the political designs attributed to her, was sent to lifelong imprisonment in the Tower.[1] Thither, too, went the Countess of Shrewsbury, "the only worker and contriver of the lady's bedlam opposition," said those who thought they discerned another Popish plot; for "though the Lady Arabella hath not as yet been found inclinable to Popery, yet her Aunt made account believe, that being beyond the seas in the hands of Jesuits and Priests, either the stroke of their arguments or the pinch of poverty might force her to the other side."[2]

Summoned before the Lords of the Privy Council, on the charge of having aided and abetted Lady Arabella's escape, Lady Shrewsbury acted with "high and great contempt" towards their lordships, saying the proceedings were "but tricks and gigs," and that as a peeress she would be tried by her peers, or not at all. To all their questions she refused to give any answer whatsoever, to the very considerable embarrassment of their lordships, who wasted much valuable time trying

[1] Lady Arabella died in the Tower, 1615.
[2] Winwood's *Memorials*.

to persuade their prisoner to be tried. Vainly they pointed out the heinousness of her conduct, but no amount of reasoning moved Lady Shrewsbury, who was ultimately sent back to the Tower, "rather upon wilfulness than upon any great matter; only the King is resolute that she shall answer to certain interrogatories, and she as obstinate to make none, nor to be examined."

Between two such stubborn people the Lords of the Privy Council had a sorry time, for the King ordered them to examine Lady Shrewsbury again, when they fared no better than on the previous occasion.

"The Countess of Shrewsburie was called before the Counsaile and Judges on Teusday at the Lord Chancellors; where by the Atturney and Sollicitor, and of all the Lords and Judges her contempt towards the King and Sollicitor, and that table was laid open and much aggravated for her refusing to answer, and scornful terms used towards some at her first conventing, and her persisting still in the same course, which example might prove of dangerous consequence, to all which she replied nothing but the privilege of her person, and a rash vow which she could not violate."[1]

Archbishop Abbott and the Earl of Northampton endeavoured to prove, "by divers texts and examples in holy Scriptures," that such a vow was contrary to divine law. Neither Lords temporal nor spiritual could move Lady Shrewsbury, who merely reiterated she had

[1] John Chamberlain's letters, July 1612.

MARY, COUNTESS OF SHREWSBURY

Reproduced by the kind permission of the Master of St. John's College, Cambridge

made a vow to reveal nothing, and it was "better to obey God than man."

Even Sir Edward Coke, the vituperative Attorney-General, fared no better, though with his usual impoliteness he called the Countess "an obstinate Popish recusant," who had "perverted also the Lady Arabella." Lady Shrewsbury paid no attention to any of them; she had said she would not answer their questions, and not one word would she say. The baffled Lords of the Privy Council, who could in no wise prevail against such a determined lady, sentenced her to be fined £20,000 and imprisonment in the Tower during the King's pleasure.

CHAPTER XV

LADY SHREWSBURY, who never forsook a
friend or forgave an enemy, went back to the
Tower in high resentment against the Earls
of Suffolk and Northampton for the unfriendly
part they had played towards her at the Council table.
The Howards were so powerful that it would have
made all the difference to Lady Arabella and her aunt
if they had used their influence for instead of against
the prisoners. By their attitude they had ranged themselves amongst those Lady Shrewsbury delighted to
hate, and upon whom she resolved to be revenged
sooner or later. At first it did not seem likely this could
ever come to pass, so mighty were the Howards, so
disgraced my Lady Shrewsbury; but the very fact of
her imprisonment ultimately proved the means which
brought about their ruin.

The Earl of Suffolk, a weak man, allowed himself
to be ruled by his wife, an avaricious, unscrupulous
woman, who used her husband's position, and her
daughters' beauty, as a means to advance the family
fortunes. The four girls were lovely even in babyhood,
especially the second one, Frances, who had "the best
nature and sweetest disposition of all her father's

children, exceeding them also in delicacy and comeliness of her person." When they reached the ages of thirteen or fourteen—"too young to consider but old enough to consent"—Lady Suffolk arranged great marriages for them, being especially pleased when she brought about a match between Frances and the fifteen-year-old Earl of Essex,[1] to whom had been restored his father's honours and estates.

The marriage took place amidst scenes of great rejoicing on January 5th, 1606, though—as usual in all child marriages—the bride and bridegroom separated after the ceremony, the boy husband to travel abroad and complete his education, whilst the girl wife returned to her mother. Nothing more unfortunate could have happened to little Lady Essex, for Lady Suffolk was the last woman to give wise guidance during the difficult transition years when her daughter grew from a child to a woman. An onlooker who afterwards became gentleman-in-waiting to the Earl of Essex told how the girl bride passed the years of her husband's absence:

"The Court was her nest, her father being Lord Chamberlain; and she was hatch'd up by her mother, whom the sour Breath of that Age (how justly I know not) had already tainted; from whom the young Lady might take such a Tincture, that ease and greatnesse, and Court Glories, would distain and impress on her, than any way wear out and diminish. And growing to be a

[1] Robert Devereux, 3rd Earl of Essex, 1591–1646. Became the famous Parliamentary general during the Civil War.

beauty of the greatest magnitude in that Horizon, was an object fit for admirers and every Tongue grew an Orator at that shrine."

Like all other girls in their teens, Lady Essex had a devoted band of "servants," young men who dedicated themselves to the service of one particular mistress whose beauty and virtues they upheld as the paragon of womanhood. Never before had women been so worshipped and courted, for reverent admiration had been replaced by humble servility which treated women as young goddesses. Glorying in their slavery, gallants besought earnestly for a favour whereby they might demonstrate to the world their thraldom: "If he get any remnant of hers, a busk-point, a feather of her fan, a shoo-tye, a lace, a ring, a bracelet of hair, he wears it for a favour on his arm, in his hat, finger, or next his heart. Her picture he adores twice a day, and for two hours together will not look off it . . . a garter or a bracelet of hers is more precious than any Saint's Relique, he lays it up in his casket (O blessed Relique) and every day will kiss it: if in her presence, his eye is never off her, and drink he will where she drank, if it be possible, in that very place, etc. . . .

"He desires to confer with some of her acquaintance, for his heart is still with her, to talk of her, admiring and commending her, lamenting, moaning, wishing himself any thing for her sake, to have opportunity to see her, O that he might but enjoy her presence! . . .

"Another he sighs and sobs, swears he hath *Cor*

194

scissum, an heart bruised to powder, dissolved and melted within him, or quite gone from him, to his mistress' bosome belike; he is in an oven, a Salamander: the fire, so scorched with love's heat; he wisheth himself a saddle for her to sit on, a posie for her to smell to, and it would not grieve him to be hanged, if he might be strangled in her garters; he would willingly die tomorrow, so that she might kill him with her own hands."[1]

Old friends saw nothing of their former comrade:

> "And now—instead of mounting barbed steeds
> To fright the soul of fearful adversaries—
> He capers nimbly in a lady's chamber
> To the lascivious pleasing of a lute."[2]

The ladies exacted almost slavish homage from their admirers, who must always be ready to man their ladies to plays at the theatres; squire them to card-parties; escort them out hunting or hawking; accompany them at shuttlecock; wait on them at bowls or archery; and partner them at balls and masks.

A gentleman spent many anxious hours practising "the tricks to make my lady laugh when she's disposed," or devising "How and which way I may bestow myself to be regarded in her sun-bright eye." Friends of his own age, but slightly more experienced, made valuable suggestions:

> "Flatter and praise, commend, extol their graces;
> Though ne'er so black, say they have angels' faces.
> That man that hath a tongue, I say, is no man,
> If with his tongue he cannot win a woman."[3]

---

[1] *The Anatomy of Melancholy*, by R. Burton.
[2] *King Richard III*, i, i.
[3] *The Two Gentlemen of Verona*, iii, i.

Sound advice doubtless, but much depended on the individual tongue; one man could not get his round a compliment anyhow, whereas they simply rippled off the end of

> "A man in all the world's new fashion planted,
> That hath a mint of praises in his brain."[1]

Such a one would greet his mistress as, "most excellent accomplished lady, the heavens rain odours on you," to the stupefication of simple country gentlemen, who, completely bedazzled by such eloquence, could only exclaim enviously, "That youth's a rare Courtier! Rain odours! Well."[2]

A really proficient servant often let his tongue run away with him, making such extravagant promises that, if the lady called on him to fulfil them, he would be bound to admit he spoke metaphorically, after the manner of lovers.

"When we vow to weep seas, live in fire, eat rocks, tame tigers; thinking it harder for our mistress to devise imposition enough than for us to undergo any difficulty imposed. This is the very monstrosity in love, lady, that the will is infinite, and the execution confined; that the desire is boundless, and the act a slave to limit."[3]

A gentleman who distrusted the efficiency of his tongue could take heart in the reflection that "much is the

---

[1] *Love's Labour's Lost,* I, I.
[2] *Twelfth Night,* III, I.
[3] *Troilus and Cressida,* III, I.

force of heaven-bred poesy," and recall Mr. William Shakespeare's advice to lovers in *The Two Gentlemen of Verona*:

> "You must lay lime to tangle her desires
> By wailful sonnets, whose composed rimes
> Should be full fraught with serviceable vows . . .
> Say that upon the altar of her beauty
> You sacrifice your tears, your sighs, your heart.
> Write till your ink be dry, and with your tears
> Moist it again, and frame some feeling line
> That may discover some integrity."

It was the ambition of every girl to have her praises sung till she became as famous as Sidney's immortal Stella, but unfortunately, every lover had not Sidney's magic pen. When, in requite for some trifling favour, a lady asked, "Will you write me a sonnet in praise of my beauty?" the gentleman, as in duty bound, promised to compose one, in so high a style "that no man living shall come over it; for, in most comely truth thou deservest it." On close application, however, he often found the task quite as difficult as eating rocks or taming tigers.

"Marry, I cannot show it in rime; I have tried: I can find out no rime to 'lady' but 'baby,' an innocent rime; for 'scorn,' 'horn,' a hard rime; for 'school,' 'fool,' a babbling rime; very ominous endings: no, I was not born under a riming planet, nor I cannot woo in festival terms."[1]

[1] *Much Ado About Nothing*, v, 2.

Luckily for the lover who could not manage "a halting sonnet of his own pure brain," or even a satisfactory love-letter, there were plenty of professional scribblers ready to compose a sonnet to a lady's eyebrows, or liken her beauties to suns, stars, moons, gold, silver, flowers, precious stones, etc.[1] Even Sir Robert Carr,[2] the King's all-powerful favourite, had recourse to his secretary, Sir Thomas Overbury, when he wanted to send love-letters to Lady Essex. The two first met at a dinner-party which the Earl of Northampton gave at his grand new house at Charing Cross. The wily old Lord Privy Seal was not slow to see that his beautiful

---

[1] Shakespeare makes fun of lovers' similes in his sonnets:

"My mistress' eyes are nothing like the sun;
Coral is far more red than her lips' red:
If snow be white, why then her breasts are dun;
If hairs be wires, black wires grown on her head.
I have seen roses damask'd, red and white,
But no such roses see I in her cheeks;
And in some perfumes is there more delight
Than in the breath that from my mistress reeks.
I love to hear her speak, yet well I know
That music hath a far more pleasing sound:
I grant I never saw a goddess go,—
My mistress, when she walks, treads on the ground:
And yet, by heaven, I think my love as rare
As any she belied with false compare."

Sonnet cxxv.

[2] Scotch favourite of James I. Created Viscount Rochester 1611, Earl of Somerset 1613. Supplanted in King's favour by George Villiers 1614. Died 1645.

niece had attracted the attention of Sir Robert Carr, and, ignoring the danger to which it exposed her, he allowed the enamoured young people to use his house as a convenient meeting-place, where they might be secure from curious eyes.

Frances jumped suddenly into womanhood in the few short weeks after the dinner-party. Her devoted servants, with their sonnets and protestations, were quickly forgotten in the overwhelming passion of real love, and now for the first time she realized the terribly binding vows which in childhood had made her the wife of another man.

At this crisis the Earl of Essex, after four years' absence, returned to England and went straight to his wife, who regarded him with horror and dismay. This strange young man demanded that she should leave her father's house, and the gaiety and excitement of London, to go with him to Chartley, his far-away country-house in Staffordshire. Fate seemed closing in on Frances, who in desperation turned to the Black Arts of sorcery—fortune-telling, crystal-gazing, and palmistry—so extensively patronized by fashionable ladies who loved to dabble in occult mysteries.

Astrologers and magicians plied a lucrative trade, some being modest about their attainments, merely claiming, "In nature's infinite book of secrecy a little I can read."[1] Whereas others boldly proclaimed, "I can call spirits from the vasty deep," and were unabashed at sceptical men scoffers, who retorted, "Why,

[1] *Antony and Cleopatra*, I, 2.

so can I, or so can any man; but will they come when
you do call for them?"[1]

Husbands looked with extreme disfavour on all this
fortune-telling business, being especially uneasy about
the questions their wives asked. Ben Jonson, who in his
play, *The Alchemist*, exposed the tricks of unscrupulous
magicians, made disquieting suggestions that married
ladies went in disguise] "to that conjurer, and this
cunning woman: where the first question is, how soon
you shall die? Next, if her present servant love her?
next if she shall have a new servant? and how many . . .
what precedence she shall have by her next match? and
sets down the answers, and believes them above the
scriptures. Nay perhaps she'll study the Art."[2]

Some women did study the Art, and made a good
thing out of it, like "cunning Mary," a Southwark
laundress, who when consulted by Lady Essex told her,
"that she was unfortunate in her marriage and born to
much trouble."

Lady Essex knew that without any telling; caught
in the toils of undisciplined love, she lost all mental and
moral control, her passion being almost daily inflamed
by the ardent love-letters composed by Overbury in
Carr's name. Mrs. Turner, a doctor's widow, who had
gained notoriety by introducing the starched yellow
ruffs which so delighted society ladies, and still grievously
offended the eye of His Majesty King James, arranged a
meeting between Lady Essex and Dr. Simon Forman, a

[1] *First Part, King Henry IV*, III, I.
[2] *The Silent Woman*, II, I.

magician who specialized in love philtres. Many were the fashionable ladies who came to Forman's house at Lambeth, but, once inside, the magician always refused to make any kind of magic till his visitors had written their true names in a book he kept for the purpose. Lady Essex complied with the usual request, and Dr. Forman supplied her with philtres and charms wherewith to increase Carr's love and alienate that of her husband.

Dr. Forman died without having accomplished the purpose for which Lady Essex paid him so heavily, and in reckless desperation she brought a nullity suit against her husband. Sir Thomas Overbury, like the rest of the social world, had little difficulty in guessing that, should the Countess win her case, she would immediately become the bride of Carr and, alarmed at the prospect of losing his influence with the favourite, he did all in his power to prevent the marriage. With "peremptory sauciness," he boasted that it was his letters which had won the lady's love for Carr, and in every way sought to defame her in his patron's eyes.

Sir Robert Carr was very angry at his secretary's interference, the more so on hearing it bruited abroad that Overbury ruled Carr, and Carr ruled the King. Both King and favourite would be glad to be rid of Sir Thomas Overbury, who was politely offered a foreign embassy. Overbury, seeing through the plan, rejected the honour point-blank, with the immediate result that he was sent to the Tower for high and great contempt in refusing to serve His Majesty.

Meanwhile the divorce proceedings went on, and

seemed, moreover, likely to terminate in the lady's favour if no untoward event occurred. The one person Lady Essex feared was Sir Thomas Overbury, who on his release from the Tower might mar all. Therefore she resolved that he never should come out again alive, and going down to Hammersmith, she consulted Mrs. Turner, "the lay-mistress of poisons," telling her the evil things he had said of her to Carr. Mrs. Turner, expressing great indignation, declared he should suffer for them, "Ay, that he should; and it is a pity that he should live to defame so honourable a lady, so well descended, to the utter disparaging of her house," and that rather than he should live she would be his "Death's man herself."

Mrs. Turner undertook to procure poisons, for well she knew a certain little shop hidden away in dark alleys behind Cornhill where a needy apothecary dispensed many unwholesome things:

> "And in his shop a tortoise hung,
> An alligator stuff'd, and other skins
> Of ill-shaped fishes; and about his shelves
> A beggarly account of empty boxes,
> Green earthen pots, bladders, and musty reeds,
> Remnants of pack thread, and old cakes of roses,
> Were thinly scatter'd, to make up a show."[1]

By wholesale bribery all kinds of poisons were smuggled into the Tower, and mixed in the prisoner's food. His servant Weston afterwards admitted: "Sir Thomas never ate white salt, but there was white arsenick put

[1] *Romeo and Juliet*, v, 1.

in it. Once he desired pig, and Mrs. Turner put into it *lapis costities*. The white powder that was sent to Sir Thomas in a letter I knew to be white arsenick. At another time he had two partridges sent him from the Court, and water and onions being the sauce, Mrs. Turner put in cantharides instead of pepper; so that there was scarce anything that he did eat but there was some poison mixed. For these poisons the Countess sent the rewards; she sent many times gold by Mrs. Turner. She afterwards wrote also to me to buy more poisons."[1]

On the 15th of September, 1613, just three days before Lady Essex gained her nullity suit, it was given out that Sir Thomas Overbury had died of natural causes. There matters might have rested, had not Lady Shrewsbury too been a political prisoner in the Tower; but there were many suspicious circumstances connected with Overbury's death, and Sir Robert Carr's marriage to Lady Essex, which caused Lady Shrewsbury to put two and two together with very plausible results. For the present she said nothing, but bided her time until she should have made all sure, and could strike a decisive blow at the house of Howard.

Though she had obtained her heart's desire and was now the wife of Carr—whom the King created Earl of Somerset in order that Frances might not lose precedence by her remarriage—she had many secret terrors to face, for the poisoners and magicians she had employed were extortionate in their blackmail. Lady Somerset bribed

[1] Weston's Examination.

them to silence, but always a black shadow of fear filled her mind, and in 1615 the menace became a reality.

Lady Shrewsbury's imprisonment was not very rigorous, and from time to time she obtained permission to return home in order to nurse her husband during illness, and it was after a dinner-party at the Shrewsburys' house that inquiries were set on foot concerning the death of Sir Thomas Overbury.

Suspicion, once aroused, increased so rapidly that King James ordered Sir Edward Coke to take the matter in hand for full investigation. Then indeed did Lady Somerset's heart fail her, for the very name of the terrible Lord Chief Justice struck terror into the hearts of all guilty persons whatsoever their estate. It did not take Sir Edward Coke long to track down the evil-doers, when he made wholesale arrest of all concerned, including the Earl and Countess of Somerset.

"The Great Oyer of Poisoning" caused a prodigious sensation, not unmixed with serious alarm to many society ladies when it became known that Sir Edward Coke had discovered the whereabouts of Dr. Forman's visitors' book and intended to have it produced in Court. Many of the late magician's clients passed sleepless nights in consequence of this report, but an unexpected accident saved their reputations, for when the book was handed up to the Lord Chief Justice, "there was much mirth made in court upon the showing this book, for it was reported the first leaf my Lord Coke lighted on he found his own wife's name."[1]

[1] Sir A. Weldon.

The Earl and Countess of Somerset were both found guilty and condemned to death, but James would not suffer his former favourite to suffer the extreme penalty, and commuted the sentence to imprisonment in the Tower. The accomplices who had supplied, or administered, the poisons felt the full rigour of the law, and in sentencing Mrs. Turner, Coke ordered that "as she was the person who had brought yellow starched ruffs into vogue, she should be hanged in that dress, that the same might end in shame and detestation."[1] Even the hangman and his assistants at Tyburn wore yellow ruffs, which brought the fashion into such disrepute that the ladies who paid their last respects to Mrs. Turner, by attending her execution in their coaches, went home resolved to banish yellow ruffs from their wardrobes.

[1] Works of Sir Thomas Overbury. Rimbault.

CHAPTER XVI

MANY people did not hesitate to say that it was the "mother vine," as they called the Countess of Suffolk, who was at the bottom of Sir Thomas Overbury's murder, and that anxiety to become mother-in-law to the King's favourite led her to aid and abet, if she did not instigate, her daughter's nefarious designs. The venality of Lady Suffolk was notorious, for, besides being in the pay of Spain to reveal State secrets, she so entirely dominated her husband that she had become Lord High Treasurer in all but name. Under her influence bribery and corruption became so rampant that Bacon compared the Treasury to a shop in the Royal Exchange, with Lady Suffolk as the proprietor, and a minor treasury official acting as apprentice, calling out, "What d'ye lack, what d'ye lack?" that the public might know government offices were for sale to the highest bidder. The scandal grew to such a pitch that in 1619 the Lord Treasurer was accused of embezzlement, his wife's name being coupled with his in the charge, as no one doubted her to be the real culprit.

The Earl and Countess of Suffolk were tried before the Star Chamber, when Sir Edward Coke, always especially bitter where women were concerned, laboured actively to secure their conviction. As the proceedings took place in private, the public could not gloat over the details as they had done in the case of the Earl and Countess of Somerset; but they heard with considerable satisfaction that the Star Chamber had imposed a fine of £30,000, coupled with an order that the Lord High Treasurer and his lady should be imprisoned in the Tower till they had discharged the fine.

The same year another public man, Sir Thomas Lake, Secretary of State, suffered disgrace for his wife's sins. In this instance the charge was a libel which was spread abroad by Lady Lake and her daughter, Lady Roos, defaming the character of the Countess of Exeter. King James personally interested himself in the matter, and being convinced of Lady Exeter's innocence he determined to call the other two ladies very severely to account. Sending for Sir Thomas Lake, he advised him to keep clear of the business; but the Secretary of State, whilst thanking the King for his consideration, replied that he could not cease to be a husband and a father, therefore he desired that his name might be included in the indictment.

The case, which occupied five days, resulted in a verdict of guilty against the prisoners, King James who was present likening the crime "to the first plot of the first sin in paradise, the lady to the serpent, her daughter to Eve, and Sir Thomas to poor Adam, whose love to his wife, the old sin of our father, had beguiled him."

Despite his tribute to his innocence, the King

deprived Sir Thomas Lake of all offices, and going on the assumption, "Why, this it is, when men are rul'd by women,"[1] never again employed him in any public capacity.

One result of these two trials was that there was a general revolt against feminine domination. Women were so used to being petted, spoilt, and worshipped, that they had come to regard men as slaves to do their bidding; moreover, not content with ordering them about, they aped and copied men in every possible way. Women had long ago taken unto themselves the coveted privilege of feathers in their hats, and once let the men evolve a new fashion, before it was out of the tailor's hands the ladies would have copied it. Next they took to cropping their hair, bought men's beaver hats, wore daggers on their hips, and, finding that farthingales greatly interfered with field sports, rode booted and breeched, when careering across country after horse and hound. It was too much: and an outcry arose that women were "a mankind generation" and wanted to "wear the breeches."

In defence of their nether garments the menaced sex rose as one man, led by the easily agitated James, who declared his intention of bringing these froward women into subjection. Sending for Sir George Calvert, appointed Secretary of State in place of Sir Thomas Lake, "The King asked him many questions, most about his wife; his answer was that she was a goode woman and had brought him ten children, and would

[1] *King Richard III*, I, i.

assure his ma^tie that she was not a wife with a witnes; this and some other passages of this kind seeme to show that the King is in a great raine of taking down high handed women."[1]

James was in dead earnest, for he had another grievance against the sex, on the score that "all the country is gotten into London, so as in time England will be only London, and the whole country be left waste." With considerable alarm he viewed the increase of population, which, if allowed to continue, might fulfil the astounding prophecy made in *London's Progress*:[2]

> "Why how now, Babell, whither wilt thou build?
> The old Holborne, Charing-Cross, the Strand,
> Are going to S. Giles'-in-the-Field:
> Saint Katerne she takes Wapping by the hand,
> And Hogsdon will to Hy-gate ere't be long.
> London has got a great way from the streame;
> I think she means to go to Islington,
> To eat a dish of strawberries and creame.
> The City's sure in *Progresse*, I surmise,
> Or going to revell it in some disorder,
> Without the walls, without the liberties,
> Where she neede feare not Mayor nor Recorder.
> Well, say she do, 'twere pretty, yet 'tis pity,
> A Middlesex Baliff should arrest the City."

If such a state of things ever came to pass it would be entirely owing to women. Left to themselves men would remain contentedly on their own country estates, but wives gave them no peace till they took a house in

---

[1] John Chamberlain's letters.
[2] Epigrams of Thomas Freeman.

London for the Term. King James, speaking his mind plainly, said, "One of the greatest causes of all gentlemen's desire, that have no calling or errand, to dwell in London, is apparently the pride of the women: for if they be wives, then their husbands, and if they be maids, then their fathers, must bring them up to London; because the new fashion is to be had no where but in London: and here if they be unmarried, they mar their marriages, and if they be married they lose their reputations and rob their husband's purses."

Once up in London the ladies, according to the Puritans, did not spend their time at all profitably; if young, they danced all night and half the day; if old, they gambled at cards all day and half the night; in middle age they combined more than a sufficiency of both vices. At any age they were all agog to visit the sights of the town:

"To see a strange outlandish Fowle,
A quaint Baboon, an Ape, an Owle,
A dancing Beare, a gyants bone,
A foolish ingin move alone,
A morris-dance, a Puppit play,
Mad Tom to sing a Roundelay,
A woman dancing on a rope;
Bull-baiting also at the Hope;
A Rimers jests, a juglers cheats,
A Tumbler shewing cunning feats,
Or players acting on the stage,
There goes the bounty of our age:
But unto any pious motion
There's little coine, and less devotion."[1]

---

[1] Henry Farley.

Husbands, who should have made a firm stand against all this frivolity, proved so deplorably weak-kneed that they allowed themselves to become "their wives' pack-horses and slaves," putting aside all business "to carry her muff, dog, and fan, let her wear the breeches, lay out, spend and do what she will, go and come, whither, when she will."[1]

One thing the ladies were quite resolved upon was to visit the Globe Theatre to see Richard Burbage, "their mortal God on earth," acting in Shakespeare's and Ben Jonson's famous plays. Moralists, who had scant patience with all this actor hero-worship, grumbled that the dramatists put all sorts of ideas into women's heads. Mr. William Shakespeare had depicted Portia, a female lawyer who would have outwitted Sir Edward Coke, and Helena, a woman doctor of skill surpassing Dr. William Paddy and the whole College of Surgeons. Ben Jonson, equally blameworthy, created the character of Mistress Overdue, "a fine female lawyer," who discharged her husband's office as Justice of the Peace.

Unless something was done, and done quickly, such things would come to pass in real life, so King James called upon the Church to support him in a campaign designed to make women obey[2] their husbands. An interested public watched the experiment, and John Chamberlain narrated the first step:

[1] *The Anatomy of Melancholy.*
[2] Some authorities say that at the marriage of King James's daughter, Elizabeth, the word "obey" was left out of the marriage service.

"Yesterday the bishop of London called together all his clergie about this time, and told them he had expresse commandment from the King to will them to inveigh vehemently against the insolencie of our women, and theyre wearing brode brimmed hats, pointed dublets, theyre haire cut short and shorne, and some of them stilettoes or poinards and such other trinkets of like moment; adding with all that if the pulpit admonitions will not reforme them he wold proceed by another course; the truth is the world is very much out of order, but whether this will mend it God knows."

The Church, which had never been backward in the cause of women's reformation, undertook the charge most willingly, so that on February 12th John Chamberlain reported progress:

"Our pulpits ring continually of the insolence and impudence of women; and to help forward, the players have likewise taken them to task; and so to the ballads and ballad singers; so that they can come nowhere but their ears tingle. And if all this will not serve, the King threatens to fall upon their husbands, parents, or friends, that have, or should have power over them, to make them pay for it."[1]

At the same time there arose a scare that men had become effeminate:

> " A woman impudent and mannish grown
> Is not more loath'd than an effeminate man."[2]

---

[1] Birch's *James I.* [2] *Troilus and Cressida*, III, 3.

Fashionable young men went about "like women in men's apparel, and smell like Bucklersbury in simple time."[1] A man of fashion spent far, far too much time regarding the perfections of his own person, for, though "it is not vain-glory, for a man and his glass to confer in his own chamber,"[2] matters had come to a pretty pass when he took to carrying one about with him.

> "In yon spruse *coxcombe*, yonn affecting *Asse*,
> That never walkes without his *Looking-Glasse*,
> In a tobacco box, or Diall set,
> That he may privately conferre with it.
> How his *Band* jumpeth with his Peccadilly[3]
> Whether his *Band* strings ballance equally;
> Which way his Feather waggs! And (to say truth)
> What wordes in utterance best become his mouth."

Then the time men spent over their clothes! "In tricking up themselves men go beyond women, they wear harlots' colours, and do not walk, but jet and dance, *hic mulier, hæc vir*, more like Players, Butterflies, Baboons, Apes, Anticks, then men. So ridiculous, moreover, we are in our attires, and for cost so excessive, that . . . 'tis an ordinary thing to put a thousand Okes and an hundred Oxen into a suit of apparil, to wear a whole Mannor on his back. What with shoe ties, hangers, points, caps and feathers, scarfs, bands, cuffs, etc., in a short space their whole patrimonies are consumed."[4]

[1] *The Merry Wives of Windsor*, III, 3. The grocers and apothecaries had their shops in Bucklersbury.

[2] *Cymbeline*, IV, I.

[3] Ruff.

[4] *The Anatomy of Melancholy*.

Well might sober-minded men exclaim, "I wot not how the world's degenerate!"

> "When comely striplings wish it were their chance,
> For Cænis' distaff to exchange their lance
> And wear curl'd perwigs, and chalk their face,
> And still are poring on their pocket-glass
> Tir'd with pinn'd ruffs, and fans, and partlet strips,
> And busks, and verdigales about their hips;
> And tread on corked stilts, a prisoner's pace,
> And make their napkin for their spitting place,
> And gripe their waist within a narrow span;
> Fond Cænis that wouldst wish to be a man!
> Whose mannish housewives like their refuse state
> And make a drudge of their uxorious mate
> Who like a cot-quean freezeth at the rock,
> While his breech'd dame doth man the foreign stock."[1]

Zealous pamphleteers wasted much ink exposing the wickedness of the modern woman, charging her with mannishness and frivolity, coupled with complete indifference to home duties, and a deliberate refusal of motherhood because children interfered with sport or pleasure. Entirely forgetful of the diatribes of Philip Stubbes in the far-off 'eighties, Jacobean reformers called upon a graceless generation to revere the virtues of its grandmothers. Grandmothers, of course, upheld the pleasing fiction of their own immaculate youth: in their young days, when Queen Elizabeth ruled the land, women were patterns of ladylike perfection. They did not paint their faces; cut their hair short; smoke pipes; dance to excess; gamble at cards; swear "good mouth-

[1] Hall's *Satires*.

filling oaths"; ride astride; wear short skirts to show off
their ankles; go to dinner-parties given by men friends
at the Apollo Tavern; or visit public theatres to fall in
love with popular actors. Grandmothers, with hands
uplifted in horror, wondered what girls of the present
day were coming to!

All in vain were efforts made to persuade the ladies that
a woman's place was the home, where her one aim should
be to gain praise as a good housewife:

"As her skill in Physicks, surgerie, Extraction
of Oyles, Banqueting-stuffe, ordering of
great feasts, preserving of all sorts
of wines, conceited secrets, Distil-
lations, perfumes, ordering of wooll
hempe, Flax, making cloth, Dying,
the knowledge of Dayries, Office
of Malting, Oats, their excellent uses in a Family, Brewing,
Baking, and all other things
belonging to an Household."[1]

For guidance, scribes outlined the perfect woman
"of great modesty and temperance"; these virtues
especially appearing in her conduct to her husband,
"wherein she shall shunne all violence, passion, humour,
coveting less to direct than to be directed, appearing
ever to him pleasant, amiable and delightful." Never
should she answer him back, for bad language, though
always uncomely in a woman, is "most monstrous and
ugly when it appears before the presence of her husband.

[1] *The English Housewife*, G. Markham.

In religion she should be upright and sincere, but not take upon herself to preach in public with "that violence of spirit, which many of our (vainly accounted pure) women do, drawing a contempt upon the ordinary ministry and thinking nothing lawful but the vantages of their own inventions, usurping to themselves a power of preaching and interpreting the Holy Word, to which only they ought to be hearers and believers, or at the most but honest persuaders, this is not the office either of good housewife or good woman."[1]

Unfortunately the ladies remained obstinately indifferent, both to housewifery attractions and the outcry against their sex. King, Church, and writers might rant and rave, but it was all to no purpose so far as women were concerned. "Faults, faults, nothing but faults," quoth Barnaby Rich, who thought he had discovered one great secret why women were so indifferent both to housekeeping attractions and their own spiritual welfare. They did not want either to live in the country or go to heaven, "because there was no good coachway!"

Coaches were the pride and joy of fashionable ladies who drove up and down the town, till London's narrow streets were "incumbered with the rumbling and rowling of coaches." Michael Drayton soundly trounced both ladies and coaches in his *Idea*.

> "How many paltry, foolish, painted things
> That now in coaches trouble ev'ry street
> Shall be forgotten, whom no Poet sings,
> Ere they be well wrap'd in their winding sheet!

---

[1] *The English Housewife.*

When I to thee Eternitie shall give,
When nothing else remayneth of these dayes,
And Queenes hereafter shall be glad to live
Upon the Almes of thy superfluous prayse;
Virgins and matrons reading then my rimes,
Shall be so much delighted with thy story,
That they shall grieve, they liv'd not in those times,
To have seene thee, their sexes onely glory:
  So shalt thou flye above the vulgar throng,
  Still to survive in my immortall song."

Then, just as in the 'eighties, grave doubts were cast on the reason why ladies went to church. Barnaby Rich feared that it was not to worship, and rather "to see new fashions than to gather good instruction, and a number of them to be seene themselves, than to seeke God."

" Now what zeale is that zeal, that will neither let slip a sermon, nor let goe a new fashion? this strange attiring of themselves may well bring admiration to fools, but it breeds laughter to the wise.

"You shall see some women goe so attired to the church, that I am ashamed to tell it out loud, but harke in your eare, I will speake it softly; they are so be-painted, so beperwigd, so bepowdered, so perfumed, so bestarched, so belaced, and so beimbroched, that I canot tell what mentall vertue they may have that they doe keep inwardly to themselves."[1]

One pastor, Robert Burton, rector of St. Thomas's,

[1] *The Honestie of this Age*, Barnaby Rich.

Oxford, even went so far as to say ladies came to church to show off their silk stockings, and once seated "they pull up their petty-coats, and outward garments, as usually they do to shew their fine stockings, and those of purest silken dye. . . . And what shall we say otherwise of that baring of their necks, shoulders, naked breasts, arms and wrists. . . ."[1]

Robert Burton knew far more than was befitting any doctor of divinity, let alone a bachelor, but, his curiosity once whetted, he asked for information concerning women, unseemly for the ears of any unmarried man:

"Why do they crown themselves with gold and silver, use coronets and tires of several fashions, deck themselves with pendants, bracelets, ear-rings, chains, girdles, rings, pins, spangles, embroyderies, shadows, rabatoes, versicolor ribbands? why do they make such glorious shews with their scarfs, feathers, fans, masks, furs, laces, tiffanies, ruffs, falls, calls, cuffs, damasks, velvets, tinsels, cloth of gold, silver, tissue? with colours of heavens, stars, planets: the strength of mettals, stones, odours, flowers, birds, beasts, fishes, and what-soever Africk, Asia, America, sea, land, art, and industry of man can afford? Why do they use and covet such novelty of inventions, such new fangled tires, and spend such inestimable summs on them? 'To what end are those crisped, false hairs, painted faces,' as the Satyrist observes, such a composed gait, not a step awry? Why

[1] *The Anatomy of Melancholy.*

218

are they like so many Sybarites, or Nero's Poppæa,
Assuerus' concubines, so costly, so long a dressing, as
Cæsar was marshalling his army, or an hawk in pruning?
. . . *A Gardiner* takes not so much delight and pains in
his garden, an horseman to dress his horse, scour his
armour, a Marriner about his ship, a Merchant about
his shop and shop-book, as they do about their faces,
and all those other parts: such setting up with corks,
streightning with whale-bones; why is it, but as a day-
net catcheth larks, to make yong men stoop unto them?
. . . But why is all this labour, all this cost, preparation, riding, running, far fetched, and dear bought
stuffe? 'Because forsooth they would be fair and fine,
and where nature is defective, supply it by art.' . . .
Why do they keep in so long together, a whole winter
sometimes, and will not be seen but by torch or candle-
light, and come abroad with all the preparation may
be, when they have no business, but only to shew themselves? why do they go with such counterfeit gait . . .
such gestures, apish, ridiculous, undecent attires . . .
use those sweet perfumes, powders and ointments in
publike; flock to hear sermons so frequent, is it for
devotion? or rather as Basil tels them, to meet their
sweet-hearts, and see fashion; for, as he saith, commonly
they come so provided to that place, with such curious
complements, with such gestures and tires, as if they
should go to a dancing school, a stage-play, or bawdy-
house, fitter then a Church."

Whilst admitting that women were "necessary evils,"

Burton strongly advised young men hovering on the brink of matrimony to withdraw whilst yet there was time, for "in sober sadness, marriage is a bondage, a thraldom, a yoke, an hinderance to all good enterprise." No matter what kind of wife a man chose there were sure to be drawbacks: if stupid he would be ashamed of her; if learned she would look down on him; if plain she would paint; if pretty be unfaithful; if poor bring misery; if rich "she will ride upon thee, domineer as she list, wear the breeches in her oligarchical government, and beggar thee besides." Happy, happy bachelors! as a thank-offering for ills escaped, Burton suggested they should found a college where unmarried "old maids" could live together.

The storm against women might have blown over in time without leaving any visible effeƈt, if King James and the reformers had not had the aƈtive co-operation of Sir Edward Coke. The Lord Chief Justice, though a terror to the world at large, had no control whatsoever over his second wife, Lady Hatton,[1] who not only refused to bear her husband's name, but flouted him in every possible way.

Whilst Sir Edward Coke resided at his chambers in the Temple, Lady Hatton lived in great state at Ely House in Holborn. Once the residence of the Bishops of Ely, it was justly famous for its lovely gardens, its

---

[1] Elizabeth, d. of Thos. Cecil, Earl of Exeter, m. Sir William Hatton.

roses and its strawberries, to which the most popular
dramatist of the day made reference :

Gloucester. My Lord of Ely!
Ely. My lord ?
Gloucester. When I was last in Holborn
    I saw good strawberries in your garden there :
    I do beseech you send for some of them.
            Richard III, iii, iv.

Lady Hatton entertained lavishly, but her husband
received no invitation to these parties, and the servants
were ordered to refuse him admittance. When the Lord
Chief Justice did come to visit his wife he had to go
round by the side door, so that Count Gondomas, who
had asked for and been refused permission to pass
through Ely House gardens, told King James "that my
Lady Hatton was a strange lady, for she would not
suffer her husband, Sir Ed. Coke, to come in at her
fore door, nor him to go out at her back door."[1]

Lady Hatton teased and provoked her elderly husband
in every way she could think of, she libelled him, dismantled his country house of furniture, and ran away
with her daughter whose marriage Coke had arranged
without his wife's approval. She called the Lord Chief
Justice "a base treacherous fellow." "The words I
cannot deny," said Lady Hatton when friends remon-
strated. After years of wrangling the unhappy couple
took their differences before the Privy Council, where
"they accused one another in a great manner." Lady
Hatton indeed declaimed against her husband so ably,

[1] J. Howell's letter.

albeit bitterly, that those who heard her said that even the famous player Richard Burbage "could not have acted better."

Coke took a bitter revenge for his unhappy domestic life, by using his unrivalled legal knowledge to lower the status of women, making invidious distinctions between the sexes which aforetime had never been thought of. The weight of his authority created a precedent whereby women's independence was first hampered, and her place in the State withheld for several generations.

Elizabethan women played an important part in the history of their generation, but passing centuries have dimmed the events which were of paramount importance in their lives. Kings and queens have become legendary, great personages forgotten, but the women of the time have attained immortality by their inspiration of Shakespeare's heroines.

APPENDIX

I

Shallow. Sir Hugh, persuade me not; I will make a Star-chamber matter of it; if he were twenty Sir John Falstaffs he shall not abuse Robert Shallow, esquire.   1–3

. . . .

Shallow. The Council shall hear of it; it is a riot.

Evans. It is not meet the Council hear of a riot; there is no fear of Got in a riot. The Council, look you, shall desire to hear the fear of Got, and not to hear a riot; take your vizaments in that.   34–38

. . . . . .

Falstaff. Now, Master Shallow, you'll complain of me to the King?

Shallow. Knight, you have beaten my men, killed my deer, and broke open my lodge.

Falstaff. But not kissed your keeper's daughter?

Shallow. 'Tut, a pin! this shall be answered.

Falstaff. I will answer it straight: I have done all this. This is now answered.

Shallow. The Council shall know of this.

Falstaff. 'Twere better for you if it were known in
  Council: you'll be laughed at.

Evans. Pauca verba, Sir John; goot worts.

Falstaff. Good worts! good cabbage, Slender, I broke
  your head: what matter have you against me?

Slender. Many, sir, I have matter in my head against
  you; and against your cony-catching rascals,
  Bardolph, Nym, and Pistol: they carried me to
  the tavern, and made me drunk, and afterwards
  picked my pocket.   107–125

  The Merry Wives of Windsor, Act i, Sc. i.

The reference to Sir John Falstaff's recent affray,
which so aroused the wrath of Justice Shallow, is usually
held evidence of Shakespeare's reputed poaching in
Sir Thomas Lucy's park at Charlecote. But it is very
unlikely that the dramatist would wish to call attention
to this escapade of his youth; nor would it have been
of any interest to his audience if he had.

Tradition says that *The Merry Wives of Windsor*
was written at Queen Elizabeth's express command,
and because she desired to see Sir John Falstaff in love.
Shakespeare is credited with having complied with
the royal request so speedily that he completed the
play in fourteen days. As might be expected, it is a
rollicking comedy, the fat knight's amorous adventures
taking place in Windsor town and forest.

There can be little doubt that the play was first
performed at one of the royal palaces, before the Queen,

her privy councillors, ladies, and other members of the Court. Such an audience would "tickle o' the sere" with laughter if the play opened with a topical allusion to a famous quarrel, the disputants being no less honourable personages than Elizabeth, Lady Russell,[1] and the Lord High Admiral,[2] Constable of the Honour and Castle of Windsor, Keeper of Windsor Forest and Seneschal of Windsor.

The dispute in question was of long standing, and, both parties being extremely obstinate, it went on for years. In 1589 Queen Elizabeth appointed Lady Russell custodian of Donnington, "a little but very neat castle, seated on the brow of a woody hill," she having "the custody of the castle with all the profits," but the Lord Admiral claimed right of residence, which was vigorously denied by her ladyship. In 1594 they, or rather their representatives, had come to actual blows, and the indignant Lady Russell threatened to make a Star Chamber matter of it, appealing to the Privy Council through the medium of her nephew, Sir Robert Cecil.

Dowager Lady Elizabeth Russell to the Council.

She has been offered great indignity by Mr. Lovelace, Lieutenant of the Forest and Castle of Windsor

[1] Elizabeth (1528–1609), one of the learned daughters of Sir A. Cooke, sister to Lady Burghley and Lady Bacon.

[2] Charles Howard (1535–1624), 2nd Baron Howard of Effingham, created Earl of Nottingham, 1596. In command of the Fleet against the Spanish Armada.

under the Lord Admiral. She came early this October to a certain copyhold, to view when certain trees had been cut down by Laurence Manfield, and Lovelace's man. And when she came to the house she called for the key, and was answered that Lovelace had it. She commanded the door to be broken open, and found two of Lovelace's men within to keep possession against her, whom she brought home to her house and set them by the heels in her porter's lodge: saying she would teach them to come within her liberties and keep possession against her, Lovelace knowing that no Sheriff has authority to enter or execute any process but by her bailiff by force of her charter. If she had offered him money the law was open to him. Hereupon about two o'clock Lovelace came with 16 halberts and long staves within the gate of her house, which is her castle, broke open the door and locks of the lodge and took out his men. She prays the Council to call Lovelace before them, that he may be committed to prison and fined: to the example of any other to offer the like to any noble woman in her own house, contrary to law and privilege of her liberties held by charter.

Cecil evidently had misgivings as to the righteousness of his aunt's case, for before presenting the appeal he consulted Sir Edward Coke, the Attorney-General, who on October 16th, 1594, wrote in reply:

"I have considered of the State of the cause between my lady Russell and Mr. Lovelace, and of the proceedings on either part, and I take it the Star Chamber

DONNINGTON CASTLE

Photo by Photochrom

is no fit court for my lady to complain in ; for, as your honour knoweth, that high court without respect striketh on both sides, and in this case, the causes so intermixed as on the one day they cannot punish Lovelace but on the other they must sentence against my lady. For, albeit an honourable lady being so abused as she was could hardly (all circumstances considered) brook such indignities, yet her stocking and imprisonment of his men is not justifiable in law, and seeing there is no great inequality of persons, I would not have them suffer equal punishment. But, if it would please you and other of the honourable lords of her Highness's Council to call Lovelace before you and let him understand the quality of his offence and, if he do not to my lady Russell's satisfaction submit himself, that then it would please you to bind him over till the matter might be more deeply examined, in my opinion it were the best and safest course for my lady."[1]

In 1600 the dispute about Donnington still being unsettled, despite "bribes wrought unconscionably to the persuasion of the Prince's heart," Lady Russell thought of a new idea, namely, to transfer her interest to her daughter, Elizabeth Russell, one of Queen Elizabeth's Maids of Honour, and evidently a favourite of the Lord High Admiral. In pursuance of this idea she wrote to Cecil:

"I thank you for your friendly letter, which I received
[1] Hatfield MSS. Hist. MSS. Commission, vol. x. p. 7.

Pleas, and sharply to take him up for doing me an open wrong, as better learned than himself affirm: he was made Justice but last term. The case is this:—In the matter between Anne Lovelace and me, their side had put in an insufficient plea: my counsel moved that they would amend their plea: They did not. Whereupon I had order in the Court that if it were not amended by such a day I should have judgment. After the term done and my counsel out of town, Mr. Justice Warberton revoked this rule, which by law he could not, being a record of court. Whereupon an horrible riot followed: a hundred coming upon my land and reaped and carried away twenty acres of wheat, thirty well weaponed persons with pikestaves and bills standing to guard the workmen, when two of my men were hurt and the rest cast down, and not suffered to carry any of my corn out of the field. I am persuaded to put up a complaint to the Lords of the Council, and am bold to acquaint you first withal. The grant she claimeth was for service done and to be done, made while she waited upon me. She went from me and refused to serve me, as appeareth by an homage, whereupon I entered and took it into my hands. She paid no fine. My counsel put this to a demurrer of Judges. Mr. Warberton, after the time of term more than he ought, revoked the order to a common issue. Good Mr. Secretary, let him know his duty since he knoweth not honesty nor justice. My being your Aunt, my place had deserved more regard of justice than to have my maiden's cause contrary to the order of the Court and after term ended, and when my counsel was out of town, to be altered. It is the first precedent that ever was heard in any court.

Your desolate wronged Aunt."[1]

Apparently Cecil took the matter more calmly than Lady Russell liked, for she soon followed up her former letter with another:

"Think that it toucheth you in honour in the face of the world to see your Aunt, a noblewoman that hath made a petition—a most just cause to the Council table to have redress against so flat a wrong offered by Justice Warberton, contrary to law, in undoing after term when he was no Justice what was done by the whole Bench and Court, so much to my disgrace as to revoke an order for judgment against Anne Lovelace, that so shamefully hath so long troubled me for recompense of my kindness, in being willing to have gotten her Mr. Latten for a husband: gave that grant *pro servitio impenso et in posterum impendendo*, which when she refused to serve me, I entered on again. If she had continued my favour her grant could not have been good longer than I lived, because I had altered the property from being a copyhold in letting it out for divers years in particulars, and that to divers, with increase of rent, being in old rent but 39s. 8d., her tenant rentall, that now is in or, paying 5 l. for one close, another 40s. for the house, and one Manfeld 24s. or 4 noble for another close. It is but a trifle

[1] Hatfield MSS. vol. xi. p. 423.

yearly. It is well known that I give away in a year 20 times the value. But I hold my honour more dear than my life. Neither list I while I breathe to be thus bearded by a girl's tearing out of my teeth what I meant to be preferment in my own parish if she had kept my favour. If she had paid any fine, there had been some reason. If herself had not been by wages and my charge during her abode with me maintained, it had been somewhat. But this in mine own manor to be cozened for my kindness, I think it too great a dishonour and disgrace for me to bear by my Lord Admiral's maintenance or Mr. Warberton's wrong. If I had presumed to inform the Council of any untruth, I might justly be blamed, and the matter shuffled up as it is. But her Majesty's pardon (for the riot done after the rule given in Court for judgment coming) before I had any relief for my just complaint made to the Lords, nor nothing done to my satisfaction of corn taken, what greater disgrace can be offered? And if justice according to law be not yielded by Justices, why be they judges? I will agree to what order yourself shall think fit for my honour removing her whom I will never leave to sue while I live. . . . These cater-pillars . . . those that deserve best of them. Confound it to my honour and equity as yourself . . . and my L. Admiral . . . whom . . . opposeth his authority against me. This done I am going to Donington."[1]

In 1602 Lady Russell was in residence at Donnington

[1] Hatfield MS. Hist. MSS. Com. xi. p. 563 (damaged).

Castle, for on the 3rd of August, hearing a report that the Queen meant to pay a visit near, she wrote to invite Cecil to stay with her:

"If it please you to lie in Donington Castle, the poor desolate widow will afford you and my lord of Worcester and his lady and my lord of Shrewsbury and his lady, your friends, three bedchambers, with inner chambers, castle fashion, the best I have."[1]

In 1603, after Queen Elizabeth's death, the Lord Admiral regained possession, greatly to the amusement of all who had watched the protracted quarrel. Sir Thomas Edmunds wrote and told the Earl of Shrewsbury:

"His L. in his passage hither by way of Neweberrieye, hath recovered the possession of Donnington Castle from the Ladye Russell, she being absent in Wales with her daughter Lady Harbert."

Another correspondent of the Earl of Shrewsbury, this time the Earl of Worcester, father-in-law of Lady Russell's daughter, likewise wrote of the matter:

"If I had paper and space I would have wryten of my Lord Admirall's taking possession of Dunington

[1] Hatfield MS. Hist. MSS. Com. vol. xii.

from my Lady Russell, and keepeth the castell and her Lady out of dores."

On hearing what had happened, Lady Russell lost no time in coming back from Wales; and this time she did make a Star Chamber matter of it:

" *La Dame Russell vers Le Countee de Nottingham Star-Chamber Riots.*[1]

"Mich. 4 Jae. In Camera Stellata, pur un Riot en Donnington Castle, and un aut en Donnington Park. Le case appiert que la Dame Russell avoit custodian castri pur sa vie ove u fee pur l'exerciser de cest office al 2d ob le jour, and fuis la Roigne Eliz. grant le Castle al Countee de Nottingham and ses heires. La Countee mista les servants ove son furniture de household a le Castle pour pparer son lodging la, and les servants del Dame Russell firme le huis encount eux and refuse de ceo ovrer, que ils ceo overont ove iron barres and enteront, and puis ils peaceablement expel les servants del Dame que eux denieront de vener eins. Et le question fiut si ceo soit riot en les servants le Countee, and pcurement en le Countee. Et resolve per Popham Chiefe Justice, Cook Chiefe Justice del Common Pleas, and Fleming Chief Baron, que n'est riot ne procuremt, quia le Castle esteant a le Countee en property, and la Dame ayant que le custody ove un salary, le Countee m fuit tour foits en possession, and le possession que la Dame and ses servants gard fuit le possession del Countee

[1] Sir Francis Moore's Law Reports, vol. lxxii.

m, and quant les servants le Countee ovont le huis and
infreint le porte ove force, ils sont forsq trespass a lour
master and nemy a Dame; issint lour assembly esteant
per le loyal Commandmt le lour Seignior, ne fuit
illoyal, ne lour entent illoyal, ne lour fact illoyal encount
la Dame, n'asciw force pair en terror, n'ascun plage
done. Et sils avoyent fait violence and battery al pson
des servants la Dame, une le Countee ne sra dit le pcurer
de ceo, quia le commandmt que il done fuit tout loyal,
que le misexecuting ne sra impute a luy, mis sil ust
done illoyal commandmt le commander respondra pur
tout que est misexecute. Quant al riot en le Park la
Dame avoit le custody del park, and le herbage and le
Countee avoit l'inheritance franwtenemt and soile de
ceo, per que les Justices avant dits agreeont q si le
keeper del Park succide les arbes, ou prist eins al agistmt
tant q ils ne relinquish herbage sufficient pur le Deere
il forfeit son Office. Issint si u ad le herbage dun part,
and surcharge le park ove tant chattel que les Deere
nont sustenance convenient il est un trespasser. Mes
pur ceo que le riot fuit suppose en le garder dun forcible
watch entviron le Lodge, and n'appiert u le lodge appent
al office del keeper, le Court ne censure cest riot. Et
nota que touts les Judges tiegnont, que si un ad le
custody dun Castle ou meason que vie, and il denia
l'owner denter en le meason, and firme le huis encounter
luy, ceo est un forfeiture del custody. Et Popham dit
que en Bank le Roy en que l'indictment fuit remove
hors del County de Berks que trove ceux servants del
Countee, queunx enter and expel les servants la Dame,

235

daver forcibly disseise and expel la Dame del custody del Castle, and les servants ayant plead non culp' al indiↄtment, per que le Court agard restitution, mes sils avoyent plead le commandmt le Countee specialment, ils avoyent fait bien, and nul restitution sroit grant."

A modern guide book[1] to Donnington gives this account of the quarrel:

"The office of Keeper of the Castle was at this period one of considerable importance; and in 1590 the Queen conferred the reversion of this appointment on Elizabeth, Lady Russell, widow of John, Lord Russell. It appears from certain proceedings in the Court of Star Chamber that Lady Russell, a lady of indomitable assurance and determination, incurred the displeasure of the Lord Admiral by felling trees in the woods, and killing deer in the park, and shortly afterwards we again find the parties seeking the interference of the law. In the latter case it is related that, in September 1603, King James and his Queen being on a progress were entertained by Sir Thomas Dolman, at Shaw House, and there not being sufficient accommodation there for the Queen's train, the Earl of Nottingham had placed his castle at the disposal of the Court. A party of the Earl's workmen were consequently sent to the Castle to make the necessary arrangements. They were, however, refused admittance by the servants of Lady Russell, who was at that time with her son [-in-law] Lord Herbert in

[1] *Donnington Castle, near Newbury, Berks*, by W. Money, F.S.A.

Wales, and were compelled to make a forcible entry. In the meantime the vigilant Lady Russell had returned, and finding she was debarred from entering the Castle returned to Newbury, and the next day with the Mayor and divers clothiers, all duly 'weaponed,' rode in the park towards the 'Lodge,' the official residence of the Keeper, which stood on the site of the present 'Castle House,' but was forbidden by the Earl's servants to enter either the Castle or the Lodge. A few days after, King James came to Sir Thomas Dolman, when Lady Russell personally petitioned His Majesty for the restitution of her supposed rights, but the Scottish Solon judiciously referred her to the majesty of the law. The result of the action which followed was unreservedly in favour of the Earl of Nottingham."

Donnington Castle was besieged during the Civil War, and only the gate-house now remains standing.

II

SHAKESPEARE AND A YORKSHIRE QUARREL

TWELFTH NIGHT

Maria. By my troth, Sir Toby, you must come in earlier o' nights: your cousin, my lady, takes great exceptions to your ill hours.

Sir Toby. Why, let her except before excepted.

Maria. Ay, but you must confine yourself within the modest limits of order.

Sir Toby. Confine! I'll confine myself no finer than I am. These clothes are good enough to drink in, and so be these boots too: an they be not, let them hang themselves in their own straps.

Maria. That quaffing and drinking will undo you:

. . . .

Maria. They that add, moreover, he's drunk nightly in your company.

Sir Toby. With drinking healths to my niece. I'll drink to her as long as there is a passage in my throat and drink in Illyria. He's a coward and a coystril, that will not drink to my niece till his brains turn o' the toe like a parish-top.

Act i, Scene iii.

Sir Toby. Approach, Sir Andrew: not to be a-bed
after midnight is to be up betimes; and *diluculo
surgere*, thou knowest,—

Sir Andrew. Nay, by my troth, I know not; but I
know, to be up late is to be up late.

Sir Toby. A false conclusion; I hate it as an unfilled
can. To be up after midnight and to go to bed
then, is early; so that to go to bed after midnight is to go to bed betimes. Does not our life
consist of the four elements?

Sir Andrew. 'Faith, so they say; but, I think, it rather
consists of eating and drinking.

Sir Toby. Thou art a scholar; let us therefore eat
and drink. Marian, I say! a stoup of wine!

.   .   .   .

(*Enter* MALVOLIO)

Malvolio. My masters, are you mad? or what are
you? Have you no wit, manners, nor honesty,
but to gabble like tinkers at this time of night?
Do ye make an alehouse of my lady's house,
that ye squeak out your coziers' catches without
any mitigation or remorse of voice? Is there no
respect of place, persons, nor time, in you?

Sir Toby. We did keep time, sir, in our catches.
Sneck up!

Malvolio. Sir Toby, I must be round with you. My
lady bade me tell you, that, though she harbours
you as her kinsman, she's nothing allied to your
disorders. If you can separate yourself and your

239

misdemeanours, you are welcome to the house; if not, an it would please you to take leave of her, she is very willing to bid you farewell.

Sir Toby. "Farewell, dear heart, since I must needs be gone."

Maria. Nay, good Sir Toby.

Clown. "His eyes do show his days are almost done."

Malvolio. Is't even so?

Sir Toby. "But I will never die."

Clown. Sir Toby, there you lie.

Malvolio. This is much credit to you.

Sir Toby. "Shall I bid him go?"

Clown. "What an if you do?"

Sir Toby. "Shall I bid him go, and spare not?"

Clown. "O! no, no, no, no, you dare not."

Sir Toby. Out o' time! Sir, ye lie. Art any more than a steward? Dost thou think, because thou art virtuous, there shall be no more cakes and ale?

Clown. Yes, by Saint Anne;[1] and ginger shall be hot i' the mouth too.

Sir Toby. Thou'rt i' the right. Go, sir, rub your chain with crumbs. A stoup of wine, Maria!

. . . .

Maria. Marry, sir, sometimes he is a kind of puritan.

Sir Andrew. O! if I thought that, I'd beat him like a dog.

Sir Toby. What, for being a puritan? thy exquisite reason, dear knight?

[1] St. Anne's Church, Blackfriars.

Sir Andrew. I have no exquisite reason for 't, but I have reason good enough.

Maria. The devil a puritan that he is, or anything constantly but a time-pleaser; an affectioned ass, that cons state without a book, and utters it by great swaths: the best persuaded of himself; so crammed, as he thinks, with excellences, that it is his ground of faith that all that look on him love him; and on that vice in him will my revenge find notable cause to work.

. . . .

Sir Toby. She's a beagle, true-bred.

Act II, Scene iii.

Sir Toby. O! ay, make up that: he is now at a cold scent.

Fabian. Sowter will cry upon 't, for all this, though it be as rank as a fox.

. . . .

Malvolio. . . . "some are born great, some achieve greatness, and some have greatness thrust upon them."

. . . .

Sir Toby. Shall I play my freedom at tray-trip?[1] . . .

Act II, Scene v.

Maria. Get him to say his prayers, good Sir Toby, get him to pray.

Malvolio. My prayers, minx!

Maria. No, I warrant you, he will not hear of godliness.

[1] A game with dice.

Malvolio. Go, hang yourself all! you are idle shallow things: I am not of your element. You shall know more hereafter.

Sir Toby. Is 't possible?

Fabian. If this were played upon a stage now, I could condemn it as an improbable fiction.

Act III, Scene iv.

Maria. Nay, I prithee, put on this gown and this beard; make him believe thou art Sir Topas, the curate: do it quickly; I'll call Sir Toby the whilst.

Clown. Well, I'll put it on, and I will dissemble myself in 't: and I would I were the first that ever dissembled in such a gown.

Act IV, Scene ii.

Clown. *Primo, secundo, tertio,* is a good play; and the old saying is, The third pays for all: the triplex, sir, is a good tripping measure; or the bells of Saint Bennet,[1] sir, may put you in mind; one, two, three.

. . . .

Fabian. Most freely I confess, myself and Toby
Set this device against Malvolio here,
Upon some stubborn and uncourteous parts
We had conceiv'd against him.

. . . .

Malvolio. I'll be reveng'd on the whole pack of you.

Act V, Scene i.

[1] The church of St. Bennet Hithe, Paul's Wharf.

At the beginning of 1602 Londoners had the opportunity of seeing a new play by William Shakespeare, for on February 2nd John Manningham, a student in the Middle Temple, noted in his diary:

"At our feast we had a play called 'Twelfth-Night, or What you Will,' much like the 'Commedy of Errors,' or 'Menechmi' in Plautus, but most like and neere to that in Italian called 'Inganni.' A good practise in it to make the Steward believe his Lady widdowe was in love with him, by counterfeyting a letter as from his Lady in generall termes, telling him what shee liked best in him, and prescribing his gesture in smiling, his apparaile, etc., and then when he came to practise making him believe they tooke him to be mad."

Various sources have been suggested for the main plot of the play, but none for the scenes between the jovial, hard-drinking fox-hunters and the Puritan steward, Malvolio. It is very probable, however, that Shakespeare got the idea from a contemporary quarrel which was tried in London shortly before the production of the play. Though the action takes place in Illyria, according to the play-bill, the reference to two London churches, St. Anne's and St. Bennet's, would enable a London audience to locate the position in the neighbourhood of Blackfriars, where lived Lady Russell and the Puritans who had successfully opposed the building of a playhouse in their locality.

It was Lady Russell's son, Sir Thomas Posthumus

Hoby, who brought the lawsuit which set all London talking in the winter of 1601–2. Sir Thomas, a townsman and a Puritan, had nothing in common with the Yorkshire Squires, who for their part returned his dislike with interest. Sir Richard Cholmley, mentioning various "cross accidents" of life, says: "A chief one was a troublesome, vexatious neighbour, one Sir Thomas Hoby, who having married a widow, the inheritor of Hackness lordship, having a full purse, no children, delighted to spend his money and time in suits. . . ."[1]

On the 26th of August Sir Richard Cholmley, William Eure,[2] and other sportsmen were out hunting in the neighbourhood of Hackness, and sent word to Sir Thomas that they desired to stay the night with him. Sir Thomas showed no cordiality at the prospect; he accused his guests of drunkenness; they accused him of lack of hospitality; and the visit resulted in a lawsuit.

In Yorkshire, Sir Thomas Posthumus would get scant sympathy, but, like his mother, Lady Russell, he counted on the influence of his powerful relative, Sir Robert Cecil. The defendants too tried to gain Cecil's ear, so that both sides of the quarrel are found among the Hatfield State Papers, though, unfortunately, the Star Chamber verdict has not been discovered.

Sir T. Posthumus Hoby to Sir Robert Cecil

1600, *Sept.* 5.—Impute my presumption to my urgent cause, which for justice' sake I cannot swallow.

[1] Memoirs of Sir Richard Cholmley.
[2] William, afterwards Lord Eure, d. at Malton Castle, 1646.

There has been some dryness in the Lord Eure (whose tenants are my next neighbours) almost ever since I was employed as a commissioner in these parts; which, if it has been for my partiality, or injustice, I desire on proof thereof to be punished; if it be for want of partiality (as I shall rather prove) I hope my wrongs will appear in time which I have sustained. On 26 August last, his son and brother came to my house at Hackness, whose visit I have related in the enclosed complaint to the Council, which I beseech you to read and to have delivered to the Council. I assure you it is not otherwise for me to remain in these parts, nor for any other but their own followers, that will fashion justice to their greatness. If the matter may come to judicial hearing, I shall prove all my complaint, and shall lay open the partial customs of these frozen parts. I crave your pardon for appealing from the Council here, which I did in respect of my Lord President's absence, to whom I have sent a copy of the misdemeanour; and in respect that our vice-President (the Lord Eure) is father, brother, and cousin to the offenders, and who has showed natural affection already in the cause. My house at Lynton, 5 Sept. 1600.

The Same to the Privy Council

1600, *Sept.* 5.—I beg leave to inform you of a great misdemeanour offered me in mine own house at Hackness by Mr. William Eure, son of the L. Eure, Sir William, his brother, and others whose names and facts are expressed in this enclosed. My suit is that the parties be bound before the Council at York to appear before your Lordships to answer my complaint, for it is not for me to serve any process upon them in these parts, in respect of my L. Eure's greatness, who is vice-President, and hath summoned me to appear at York, to exhibit my complaint, though he is father, brother, and cousin, to the offenders. If you shall please to send commission to the Bishop of Lymryke, Mr. Heskett, and Dr. Bennett to examine my witnesses, your Lordships shall find somewhat more than I can deliver at this instant. I shall easily derive this outrage against me conceived from envy and malice for want of partiality in me in the executing of my place and calling. From my house at Lynton in the East Riding of Yorkshire, 5 Sept. 1600.

The Enclosure.

The manner of the riotous assault on Sir Thomas Posthumus Hoby, Knight, at his house at Hackness in the N. Riding of Yorkshire, by William Eure, Sir William Eure, Richard Cholmley, William Dawny, William Hylliarde the younger, Stephen Hutchenson, and —— Smyth, yeoman falkner to the L. Eure.

On Tuesday the 26th Aug. Sir Thomas Hoby was standing in his hall at Hackness, when there came in Sir W. Eure's footboy and said that his master and sundry other gentlemen would come that night. Sir Thomas answered that he was sorry, his wife was ill

and he not so well provided for them as he wished, and
desiring the footboy to tell his master as much, he
answered that his master was hunting in the forest of
Pyckering Lythe, so he knew not where to find him.
About two hours after, the above-named, Mr. Dawny
excepted, came to Hackness with sundry other servants
and boys, and Sir Thomas hearing they were come into
his dining-room went to them and told them they were
welcome. Presently after this Sir William Eure's footboy took forth cards and laid them on the table, wherewith some of the gentlemen exercised until supper.
In the beginning of supper, Mr. Eure pretending he
had come to hunt, Sir Thomas sent for his servant that
had charge of his deer, who dwelt three miles from him,
to come the next morning, and so continued with them
all the time at supper, which was spent by the gentlemen
partly in discoursing of horses and dogs, sports whereunto Sir Thomas never applied himself, partly with
lascivious talk where every sentence was begun or
ended with a great oath, and partly in inordinate
drinking unto healths, abuses never practised by Sir
Thomas. In supper-time came in a footboy whom they
had sent for Mr. Dawny, and brought word he would
come in the morning. After supper Sir Thomas willed
to have their chambers made ready, and came himself
to bring them to their lodgings, but they being at dice
told him they would play awhile, so he did leave them
and went down and set his household to prayers as
they were accustomed. When Sir Thomas and his
family had begun to sing a psalm, the company above

made an extraordinary noise with their feet, and some of them stood upon the stairs at a window opening into the hall, and laughed all the time of prayers. The next morning they went to breakfast in the dining-room, and Sir Thomas hearing them call for more wine, sent for the key of the cellar and told them they should come by no more wine from him. Presently Sir Thomas sent to Mr. Eure to know how he would bestow that day, and told him if he would leave disquieting him with carding, diceing, and excessive drinking, and fall to other sports, they should be very welcome. After this message Mr. Eure sent to Sir Thomas's wife that he would see her and begone, whereunto she answered she was in bed and when she was ready she would send him word. At his coming she prayed him to depart the house in quietness, and going to the rest of the company, he called a servant of Sir Thomas, and said, "Tell thy master he hath sent me scurvy messages, and the next time I meet him I will tell him so, if he be upon the bench, and will pull his beard!! Coming to the uttermost court Mr. Eure said he would go to the top of the hill and fling down mill-stones and would play young Devereux, at the same time throwing stones at the windows and breaking four quarrels of glass.

Sir T. Posthumus Hoby to Sir Robert Cecil

1600, *Sept.* 26.—Details of proceedings taken before Lord Eure, the Vice-President, Sir William Mallory (whose eldest son married Lord Eure's sister), Mr.

Heskett, Mr. Stanhope, Mr. Bevercoats, Mr. D. Bennett, and Mr. Fearne. Hoby was charged with wronging certain gentlemen, unnamed, by charging them to the Council with bearing murderous minds, with committing atheistical contempts, and to have exceeded in drink. A pacification was arrived at, which resulted in the gentlemen protesting their innocence of the matters imputed, and that they never meant anything in disgrace of Hoby's wife.

The following passage occurs: "The Lord Eure told me a long tale of Duello, and that your Honour, whom he knew to be my most honourable friend, would but make the matter a jest to be sport at: for that you made sport with his son Will Eure about the last unkindness between us, that fell forth the last year, about his son's bringing cards into my house: in which matter he told me before all the Council that your Honour did make his son imitate my preacher, by using such gestures as my preacher did use in his evening exercises, and that your Honour did laugh very heartily at it." —York, 26 September 1600.

Ralph, Lord Eure, to Sir Robert Cecil

[1600–1], *Jan.* 16.—You know how Sir Thomas Hobbye is renewing before the Star Chamber, the complaint which he made before the Council at York, against my son and other gentlemen, for having misconducted themselves in his house. Be pleased to read the truth, which my son, the bearer, did affirm before this Council.—Inglebye, this 16th January.

The Enclosure.

Statement by William Eure of such things as passed in Sir Thomas Hobie's house in August last, whereupon myself and divers other gentlemen then in my company are drawn in question in the Star Chamber.

Being myself accompanied with six other gentlemen hunting at that time near to Sir Thomas Hobie's house in Yorkshire, and purposing to lodge with him in kindness, I sent beforehand my footman to signify so much unto him, and some three hours after we followed. Finding none of his servants ready to receive us, we sent our horses into the town, and went into the house ourselves. First, into the hall where we found nobody. Then into the great chamber, where we stayed some quarter of an hour or more before Sir Thomas came to us, which seemed to us strange and not answerable to our northern entertainments. Coming at last he bade us coldly welcome, and accompanied us till after supper, when he retired to his chamber. We fell to cards to beguile the time and continued to play the longer for that none of his servants came to show us any lodgings. At last, being sleepy, and understanding that his servants had been at prayer in the hall under the great chamber where we were, and were gone to bed, we were forced to seek out lodgings, which we found prepared, and so we rested that night. The next day we rose early to hunt, and word was brought by one of his servants that breakfast was ready. Whereupon I willed one of his men to entreat Sir Thomas' company, who returning answered that Sir Thomas was not yet stirring; so to breakfast we went. Which being done, we fell again to play, expecting Sir Thomas' coming forth. Shortly after one of his servants came and told me peremptorily our play was offensive to his lady, and therefore willed us to depart the house. I told him our stay was only to take leave, and he repeating the former words, I said the message was a scurvy message, and willed the servant to tell Sir Thomas I would gladly speak with him before I went. I wished to understand whether the message had proceeded from him, or that the fellow of himself had abused us. Whereupon the servant departed, and presently returning told me my lady was willing to speak with me, and guided us into an inner room next adjoining to her chamber. I going into my Lady, the others withdrew themselves into the great chamber again. Sir Thomas Hobie had shut himself into the study, being unwilling to be spoken with, but watching there, as now I may conjecture, to take advantage if I should use any unseemly speeches. I expostulated a little with my Lady about the message and entertainment, whereupon she, with some show of dislike of her husband's strange fashions, entreated me with patience to depart. Which accordingly we did, and going out of the court in some discontent, I took up a little stone and cast it towards the house, not touching any windows, and so I took horse. His suggesting of tearing any commission is merely untrue, neither was any man's heels tript up, as he incerted.

Sir Thomas Posthumus Hoby to Sir Robert Cecil

1600-1, *Feb.* 10.—Understanding that Richard Cholmly, son and heir apparent of Henry Cholmly, Esq., one of the outrageous defendants to my bill in the Star Chamber, is apprehended as one of the rebellious Earl's assistants, and hearing that his friends would have it thought that he was there by chance, and that he was a man of no power, I thought it my duty to certify your Honour my knowledge of him.

For himself, he is able, within the liberty whereof his father is bailiff by inheritance, to raise 500 men, if they should show themselves as traitorous as they do already show themselves disobedient unto her Majesty's laws. He is able to raise some of his confining neighbours where his living, named Groman Abbey (a place famous for priests), doth lie. For his estate, his father hath some 1000 marks by year entailed upon him and his heirs males. All which lieth in the most dangerous parts of Yorkshire for hollow hearts, for popery. The most part thereof with his chief house, lieth along the sea coast, very apt to entertain bad intelligenced strangers. All this estate is part in his possession upon his marriage, and part is to come to him in reversion after his father, which his father cannot otherwise dispose of, and this young man hath issue.

The reason that moved him to assist the rebellious

earls were, I think, his father's desperate estate, who doth owe more than he can pay, his backwardness in religion and to embrace civil government, and his alliance and love to the Earl of Rutland.—This 10 of Feb. 1600.

P.S.—Henry Cholmly, father to this Richard, doth claim to have the mustering of her Majesty's subjects within the liberty of Whitby Strand, and hath taken my warrants which I have sent forth for her Majesty's service, I being the commissioner for musters, and did send forth warrants in his own name by virtue of his bailiwick, when he was not commissioner.

Ralph Lord Eure to Sir Robert Cecil

1601, Oct. 19.—Give me leave, by the presenting of this and this messenger, to recommend all in one, my promise of faith, my service in my son, and the remembrance of all thankfulness for your favours to my dear brother, Sir William Eure.—Mantor, xix. October 1601.

Sir T. Posthumus Hoby to Sir Robert Cecil

1601, Oct. 29.—I have presumed (in a cause whereon my poor credit doth wholly rely) to fly unto you for assistance and redress. And because you shall see my cause is honest and my wrongs sustained too injurious to be smothered, I send here enclosed a short brief of my whole complaint, according unto my proofs

253

already published. And although I might have been not a little discouraged by some reports published in the country by Mr. William Dawny, Mr. Richard Cholmly (two of the defendants), and their friends, how far you were satisfied by them in the cause; yet resting very assured of your just inclination, I assure myself you ill afford me your favourable countenance, according to the uprightness of my honest cause, how far soever the same hath been formerly extenuated by any.— 29 October 1601.

Proofs made by Sir Tho. Posthumus Hoby, Knight, plaintiff, against William Eure, esquire, and others, defendants.

[1601].—Plaintiff is a commissioner of peace in the North and East Ridings of Yorks; of oyer and terminer; for ecclesiastical causes; for musters; and thrice a commissioner for subsidy. On August 26, 1600, defendants came to his house at Hackness, Yorks, and were well entertained by him, notwithstanding which, they committed many foul misdemeanours and outrages: namely, in making rude and strange noises in the nature of "a black santes" as it is termed, when the plaintiff's family were at prayers: in bringing cards and dice: in excessive carousing and charging the plaintiff to drink healths, contrary to his disposition: in sending word that they would set horns at his gate, and pull him by the beard: saying that they would keep his house by force: throwing his servants forth: calling the plaintiff "scurvy urchin," and "spindle-shanked ape": and divers other reproachful names, in the presence of his wife: breaking glass windows; threatening to fire the town and pull down the parish church: breaking the common stocks, &c. These outrages were grounded upon unkindness formerly conceived by Lord Eure against the plaintiff, and for malice for service done by the plaintiff by virtue of his several commissions.

Ralph Lord Eure to Sir Robert Cecil

[1601–2], *Jan.* 16.—Our house will be ever bounden to you for your favours to myself and my son. As to the slanderous bill which Sir Thomas Posthumus Hobby is preferring against us before you and the honourable Council in the Star Chamber, I entreat you to suspend your judgment till the first of this term, when the cause is to be opened, and I shall be pressed in defence of my honour to present the true state of the cause to the open view of the world, which hitherto I have forborne to do in regard of yourself and some other of his friends. If it might stand with your liking to vouchsafe your presence then, I should be happy of so honourable trial.— Birdsall, the 16th of January.

Sir Thomas Posthumus Hoby to Sir Robert Cecil

1601–2, *Jan.* 26.—Requesting Cecil's presence in the Star Chamber on the morrow, when the rude and savage wrongs and injuries inflicted on Sir Thomas by Lord Eure's family are to be considered.

255

Sir Thomas Posthumus Hoby to Sir Robert Cecil

1602, *April* 13.—I have been so ever bound to your Honour that I have presumed to present my duty and service, etc.

INDEX

INDEX

Renialme, Ascanius de, 16, 50.
Rich, Barnaby, 216, 217.
Rich, Penelope, Lady, 28, 60, 61, 62, 72–83, 84, 100–10, 111, 113, 114, 115, 116, 117, 118, 124, 125, 127, 135, 136, 158, 161.
Rich, Robert, Lord, 28, 73, 78, 79, 81, 82, 125.
Russell, Ann, 23, 25, 233.
Russell, Elizabeth, 23, 25, 227, 228.
Russell, Elizabeth, Lady, 10, 11, 12–27, 40, 44, 50, 51, 52, 70, 88, 89, 223–37, 244.
Russell, John, Lord, 10, 236.

S

Seymour, William, 186, 188, 189.
Shakespeare, William, 49, 84, 112, 187, 197, 211.
Shrewsbury, Elizabeth, Countess of, 128, 179, 180.
Shrewsbury, George, Earl of, 179, 180.
Shrewsbury, Gilbert, Earl of, 179, 180, 182, 233.
Shrewsbury, Mary, Countess of, 128, 178, 179, 180, 181, 182, 186, 187, 188, 189, 190, 191, 192, 203, 204, 233.
Sidney, Barbara, Lady, 53–71, 77, 79, 94, 95.
Sidney, Betty, 64.
Sidney, Elizabeth, 62.
Sidney, Katherine, 58, 64.
Sidney, Mary, 5⌈, 59, 64.
Sidney, Philip, Sir, 29, 60, 72–77, 85, 144, 197.
Sidney, Robert, 60–2, 79, 171.
Sidney, Robert, Sir, 38, 40, 53–71, 91, 117, 118.
Sidney, Thomas, 29, 31, 32.

Sidney, William, 58, 59, 64.
Somerset, Frances Howard, Countess of, 192, 193, 194, 198–205, 207.
Somerset, Robert Carr, Earl of, 198, 200, 201, 203, 204, 205, 207.
Southampton, Elizabeth, Countess of, 80–3, 84, 100, 119–25, 155.
Southampton, Henry, Earl of, 80–3, 86, 88, 100, 114, 117–25, 150.
Spenser, Edmund, 138, 144, 177.
Stanhope, Mr., 34, 35.
Stanhope, Thomas, Sir, 180, 181.
Stubbes, Philip, 4, 5, 6, 7, 214.
Stuart, Arabella, 126, 128, 158, 161, 181, 182, 183, 186, 187, 188, 189, 191, 192.
Suffolk, Countess of, 153, 192, 193, 206, 207.
Suffolk, Earl of, 132, 141, 152, 192, 206, 207.

T

Throckmorton, Elizabeth. See Lady Raleigh.
Tresham, Francis, 116.
Turner, Mrs., 200, 201, 202, 203, 205.

W

Walsingham, Frances. See Countess of Essex.
Walsingham, Lady, 87, 88.
Warberton, Justice, 229–31.
Warwick, Ambrose, Earl of, 140.
Warwick, Ann, Countess of, 57, 63, 64, 66, 108, 111, 138, 139, 140, 141, 143, 147, 148, 149, 150, 152, 153, 156, 157.
Whyte, Roland, 56–70, 91, 100.
Worcester, Earl of, 113, 167, 233.